Paupers and Scholars

The Transformation of Student Life

in Nineteenth-Century New England

Paupers and Scholars

The Transformation of Student Life

in Nineteenth-Century New England

DAVID F. ALLMENDINGER, JR.

UNIVERSITY OF DELAWARE

ST. MARTIN'S PRESS   NEW YORK

For Susan

Acknowledgments

To friends and teachers who read and criticized, I owe my most long-standing debts. Paul Mattingly, Charles Bowden, Jack Wilson, Susan Allmendinger, William R. Taylor, Norman Levy, Donald Scott, Joan Scott, Alan Lawson, Stanley Elkins, Theodore Baird, and James Axtell may now collect their due sum of thanks. I want to thank especially Merle Curti for his advice and direction, freely given.

To the Davis Center for Historical Studies I owe thanks for a year's time to complete research and writing. Colleagues at the Davis Center, G. Howard Miller, Arthur Zilversmit, Gerald Strauss, Selwyn Troen, Lawrence Stone, and James McLachlan, contributed immeasurably through sharing their own work and offering their criticism of mine.

Susan Strasser helped me devise ways of studying students in large numbers; and Mary Pratt Grant, Faith Foss Monti, and Patricia Turbovich helped with the study of ages. In the libraries and archives of New England I have creditors everywhere. In particular, I must thank Mrs. Evelyn Vradenburg of the Congregational Library, Richard Phillips and Miss Rena Durkan of the Amherst College Archives, and Stanley Greenberg of Forbes Library in Northampton. Atherton Parsons, of Southampton, Massachusetts, gave me generous amounts of his time and knowledge, which made possible my study of his beautiful home town.

The editors of the *History of Education Quarterly* and the *Journal of Social History* have kindly permitted me to use material originally published in those journals in different form.

Contents

List of Illustrations

List of Tables

Introduction

Students as Inarticulate People

These were a rough-hewn, heavy set of fellows, from the hills and woods in this neighborhood,—great unpolished bumpkins, who had grown up farmer-boys, and had little of the literary man, save green spectacles and black broadcloth (which all of them had not), talking with a broad accent, and laughing clown-like, while sheepishness overspread all, together with a vanity at being students.

Nathaniel Hawthorne, 1838

New England colleges acquired wealth in the decades after the Civil War, and in those high Victorian years assumed a physical and social character conveying a particular impression of their past. In their architecture and landscaping, their songs and monuments and myths, they took on the air of traditional institutions with ancient and venerable histories. Their students, the elite of a nation, could live in luxury. Yet most of the venerated colleges between 1860 and 1900 were not old. The solid new Gothic and Georgian structures and the atmosphere of continuity and tradition were false to the collective past of the colleges and their students.

During the first half of the nineteenth century, the New England colleges, like many of their students, were poor. As institutions, the colleges functioned not merely as conservative instruments of inherited culture, but as innovators as well. Their practice was one of departure and invention, not repetition. They had little money or patience for retrospective architecture or elegant plantings, and appealed to students very different from those produced by the wealthy Victorian elite. Poor boys—most of them farmer boys—had come to college earlier in the century, working toward degrees that would launch them, hope-

1

fully, into learned professions far different from anything their fathers or grandfathers had known.

Nathaniel Hawthorne (Bowdoin, 1825) knew from his own college days what those earlier students had been like. He observed them in his travels through New England and he wrote about them in his first novel. In 1838 he saw them at commencement in the Berkshires, at Williams College: "Country graduates,—rough, brown-featured, schoolmaster-looking, half-bumpkin, half-scholarly figures, in black ill-cut broadcloth,—their manners quite spoilt by what little of the gentleman there was in them."[1]

At country towns like Williamstown, Massachusetts, and Middlebury, Vermont, new colleges had been raised after the period of the American Revolution. Through the middle of the nineteenth century, they attracted young men like Hawthorne's bumpkins, whose manner suggested the schoolmaster rather than the gentleman and whose appearance betrayed rustic origins and poverty.

In their recruitment and in their management of student life, the new colleges brought about a radical and largely unwanted change in the policies of the institutions of higher education. Harvard and Yale were special cases (though even they did not escape the transformation of the antebellum decades or the denials of the post-Civil War generation), but in the New England colleges founded between 1760 and 1830 change was more obvious and the later shift from innovation to veneration even more ironic.

Everything we know about the history of colleges and universities in America identifies the nineteenth century as a time of overwhelming change. Even the presidents and professors who, after midcentury, began to write affectionate chronicles of their colleges—even these men knew that change had taken place. They wrote stories of progress from the difficult, early years down to a time when their schools had established themselves as orderly institutions, for which the weight of tradition suppressed all memory of past troubles. But because they had to create respectability and tradition, their chronicles obscured the force of change.

As celebrants of tradition they triumphed. They, along with the Victorian architecture, the landscaping, and the affluence, have shaped our conception of the past. Their achievement survived a cycle of historical revision and influenced the work of later historians whose intentions were critical rather than congratulatory. When Richard Hofstadter examined the antebellum colleges, he also found tradition-laden institutions, but he viewed them with an attitude different from that of the early collegiate chronicler. In his work, the colleges became retrogressive little institutions, clinging to a dated curriculum and a collegiate structure that stifled intellectual inquiry. As Hofstadter and his heirs saw it, it was the rise of great universities late in the nineteenth century that brought significant change to American higher education. In fact, Hofstadter regarded the end of that century as a period of "revolution" in higher education.[2]

Almost everything we know about the history of higher education between 1800 and 1900 has come down through the perceptions of academicians, founders, and reformers—men who left great collections of personal and literary documents. Important, articulate men, they experienced the establishment of the colleges and the creation of the universities. Responding to forces within their institutions, the academic reformers, in particular, have come to be seen as the agents of change.

Yet other agents were also at work, responding, in New England at least, to changes in society. They were the silent people of higher education: the students. From their point of view, the revolution in higher education in New England began very early in the nineteenth century. In terms of the experience of students, colleges between 1800 and 1860 were places of dynamic change, undergoing a structural transformation common to many other institutions throughout the northern states in this period. As far as student life was concerned, what came late in the century was a denial of earlier developments, a kind of counterrevolution.

Growth of the Student Population

One source of institutional change was the growth of the New England student population. Harvard and Yale had produced an almost constant number of graduates between 1750 and 1800, a period of stable enrollment. The number of students in all New England did rise slowly during the second half of the eighteenth century, but almost all of this increase affected the new colleges founded after the 1760s. It was not until the early nineteenth century that American higher education embarked on a period of really lasting expansion. In the decade 1751-60, New England produced 544 college graduates. A century later, between 1851 and 1860, it produced about five thousand, and between the decades ending in 1800 and 1860 the number of students graduating in the region tripled (see Table 1).[3] Although on a much smaller scale, New England was experiencing what Germany and England were concurrently experiencing—a rapid and sustained growth in its student population. Nearly all that growth came after 1800, and most of it took place—as in the eighteenth century—in the new colleges.

Causes of the Growth

Between 1800 and 1860, the population of New England increased two and one-half times, from 1.2 million to 3.1 million. Inevitably, this regional growth created a large reservoir of young men who might become students, establishing the basic demographic condition for growth in the student population. Yet the number of students (still only a small percentage of young males) increased even faster than the whole population. This was not the static student population that historical tradition has assumed.[4] The expansion of the American population across the continent and into the cities created an unprecedented demand for college graduates, especially for teachers to fill new classrooms and ministers to occupy vacant pulpits. This demand, in turn, became the positive cause of growth in the student population, an American analog to European imperial expansion and the role it played in creating job opportunities for university graduates.

At the same time, the number of schools and academies increased. Together with the phenomenon of the Second Great Awakening, when hundreds of young men pledged themselves to the ministry, these forces enlarged the reservoir of literate young men who might present themselves to the colleges.

Individual motives of a severely vocational nature propelled the growth in student numbers. The movement into the colleges did not spring primarily from an old elite sending larger numbers of its sons to college for the sake of class convention or family tradition, or to prepare them for new roles in a changing society. Nor did it result from any new intellectual taste for a literary and classical education for its own sake. Instead, the impetus came primarily from families who had never before sent their sons to college, but whose sons now enrolled to acquire the prerequisites for a professional career. Hence, the preponderance of New England graduates in teaching, preaching, medicine, and the law (which often led to jobs in new local bureaucracies).[5] Opportunities in these traditional fields expanded precisely at a time of demographic crisis in rural New England.

A negative cause, or push factor, also had begun to influence the lives of young men in the late eighteenth century. The appearance of larger numbers of students, therefore, involved something more radical than a simple growth in the whole population. The students were drawn from singular segments of New England society. They did not come primarily from the region's growing cities; they did not represent the new commercial, industrial, and working classes, or immigrant groups. They came overwhelmingly from agricultural communities, where most people still lived, but where a decline in farming was forcing the young to leave their native hills and woods. New England's country colleges grew the most rapidly, and they drew their students disproportionately from among the rural Yankees. The increase in student numbers did not result from new economic prosperity in the region. On the contrary, it came at a time of hardship, a time of declining local opportunity and economic difficulty even among respectable farm families.

Consequences of Growth

Collegiate growth in New England—and throughout America—followed a distinct pattern. The new student population was poor, too poor to afford long and expensive journeys to New Haven and Cambridge. This meant that the increasing numbers of students could not be concentrated at Yale or Harvard. New colleges literally had to meet their clientele on its own ground. And so, there was a proliferation of colleges as well as of students, colleges that would remain numerous, scattered, and, by European standards, small, until late in the nineteenth century.

These colleges were forced to compete for students by cutting the costs of higher education, a variable affecting the size of all student populations.

The need to reduce costs meant that certain amenities of student life could not survive in New England. All colleges—even Harvard and Yale—had to provide for a spare sort of student life, Spartan even by New England standards, closer to the kind of existence led by students in the universities of Scotland. Tight budgets caused certain assumptions about the nature of collegiate life to disappear between 1800 and 1860, and lower costs opened college doors to unprecedented numbers of young men without means.

The study that follows focuses on two related aspects of the transformation in nineteenth-century New England: the effect of social change upon collegiate institutions, and its effect upon student life. It introduces, though it does not explore, the topic of the impact of change upon the actual content of education. It does not deal directly with the impact of such change upon the cultural and social history of New England, in the formation of elites, or the relation between education and economic growth. Its focus remains on changes immediately affecting the material existence of students and on student life in the first half of the nineteenth century.

In a sense, any work dealing with students in a society like that of New England in this period deals with an elite. Of all the young men in the region, these students—despite the frequent incidence of poverty among them—were a small, privileged fraction. Still, they were too numerous to treat exactly as one would treat a parliament, too varied and numerous to study as one would study a few hundred noblemen or university officials. Students are the most difficult members of a collegiate community to study. A book about students does not deal directly with the articulate classes of the collegiate community—its faculty and officials. For the historian, students are a silent people.

To deal with them historically—to see who they were, what they experienced, and how they altered their institutions—the historian must use a variety of the strategies of social history to penetrate what has come to be called the history of the inarticulate. This is particularly true in the case of the young men who occupy the center of this book, and similar young men described by Nathaniel Hawthorne during the 1838 commencement at Williams: the poor, unpolished scholars from the farms and hills of old New England.

Notes

1 Nathaniel Hawthorne, *Passages from the American Note-books of Nathaniel Hawthorne* (Boston: Houghton Mifflin Company, 1883), pp. 162-64.
2 Richard Hofstadter, "The Revolution in Higher Education," in *Paths of American Thought*, ed. Arthur M. Schlesinger, Jr., and Morton White (Boston: Houghton Mifflin Company, 1963), pp. 269-90.
3 See also Arthur M. Comey, "The Growth of New England Colleges," *Educational Review* 1 (1891): 213; idem, "Growth of the Colleges of the United States," ibid. 2 (1892): 124.
4 For the decade ending in 1790, New England colleges produced one graduate for every 6,495 persons in the region. During the decade 1831-40, there was at least one new graduate for every 2,560 persons. The ratio fell throughout the early nineteenth century and continued its decline after 1860. These statements are based on U.S. Census enumerations and published registers of college graduates. Arthur M. Comey's studies, focusing on the period 1850-90, revealed a growth in all New England colleges far exceeding "their natural constituency," even among institutions drawing students from "slow-growing communities." Comey attributed the growth to

native New Englanders, not to students coming from outside the region. See Comey, "Growth of New England Colleges," pp. 213, 216-18. Cf. Laurence R. Veysey, *The Emergence of the American University* (Chicago: University of Chicago Press, 1965), p. 4; Hofstadter, "Revolution," p. 273.

5 Bailey B. Burritt, *Professional Distribution of College and University Graduates*, U.S. Office of Education Bulletin no. 19 (Washington, D.C.: Government Printing Office, 1912), pp. 62-114.

PART I

Scholars Who
Were Not Gentlemen

Within the small New England colleges of the early nineteenth century, there occurred a social transformation that would alter the entire student experience. Unlike the conscious reforms introduced with the rise of universities after the Civil War, this transformation proceeded without plan. No theorist designed it according to conscious pedagogical aims, and no institution anticipated or controlled the course of change between 1800 and 1860. Only after 1840, when New England colleges had already assumed new forms, did an awareness of the changes develop. The material conditions of an earlier collegiate life, the communal arrangements that once controlled the behavior and intellectual activity of students, had disappeared, leaving a strange disorder. These developments came in the aftermath of social change throughout the whole region. A fundamental demographic movement was under way in New England, a movement that profoundly affected the society and its institutions of higher education. Long before the rise of universities, antebellum colleges were being changed through the needs and workings of the student population itself.

1 Infiltration
by the Poor

If the New England farmer's life were a loved and lovable thing, the New England boys could hardly be driven from the New England hills. . . . An inquiry at the doors of the great majority of farmers would exhibit the general fact, that the brightest boys have gone to college, or have become mechanics, or are teaching school, or are in trade, or have emigrated to the West.

Atlantic Monthly, 1858

Poor young men, sometimes described as "needy" or "indigent" or even "paupers," gathered in large numbers in the colleges of New England during the years between 1800 and 1860. They came down from the hill towns, where opportunities were few, to the small colleges at Hanover or Williamstown or Brunswick. Even before New York State and Ohio drew many of their kind to the West, they began to infiltrate—almost imperceptibly at first—the student population. They did not want new farm lands, nor would they try to find places at home as hired workers in an agricultural proletariat; they joined, instead, a rural intelligentsia of students and teachers aspiring to the middle-class professions. By the early nineteenth century their numbers were sufficient to make men conscious of what was happening: New England society was producing a scattered, significant group of paupers and scholars. They were not paupers in the sense that they came from a clearly defined social class or had spent their youth in almshouses or begging door-to-door. Nor did they come, necessarily, from the lowest levels of society, though many, in fact, were drawn from its poorest members. More simply, they were students who had to take charity or support themselves with their own work, since their families were too poor to pay college expenses.[1] Their mere presence transformed the institutions of higher education in New England and established a new kind of student life.

One clear sign of the presence of the poor was the increasing maturity of the student population. Unlike collegiate societies of the early eighteenth or twentieth centuries, this new one was characterized by students of mixed ages. Men in their middle twenties now enrolled in large numbers, along with boys in their early teens. At colonial Harvard and Yale, almost every class had contained a few mature students, but they were exceptions—a mere 8.6 percent of the graduates between 1751 and 1760—and they usually ranked low both because of their maturity and humble origins. Colonial families commonly expected sons to enter college by seventeen or eighteen and finish by twenty-three at the very latest.[2] Older students remained few until the late eighteenth century, when student society began to include men of greater and more varied age in a trend that ceased only at the end of the nineteenth century. Between 1760 and 1860, mature students—men who entered college after their twenty-first birthdays and graduated after their twenty-fifth—increased both in real numbers and as a percentage of the whole student population (see Table 1). Between 1830 and 1860, about one-fourth of all graduates in New England were over twenty-five; at the new colleges this proportion reached one-third.[3] For some reason, more and more young men who had lagged behind their classmates in enrolling for a higher education now began to go to college.

The appearance of older students represented far more than a shift in custom or a new casualness towards the proper phasing of student careers. The laggards had not waited idly to complete their education until fancy struck. They had been delayed. Fathers had denied them freedom until they reached twenty-one, keeping them at work on the farms; or the sons themselves had held back, working and teaching school to save tuition money. Many had started trades and then, having changed their minds, had continued in their work to get money for education. This brought about a mixing of the social classes as well as ages; for the laggards in New England, like those in Europe for centuries, were the poor.[4]

Infiltration by the poor began in the late 1760s, when the first new colleges were founded in New England. Throughout most of the colonial period, Harvard and Yale had stood alone. Then, between 1765 and 1820, there arose eight new colleges, provincial institutions much closer geographically to the hill towns and the rural poor (see Table 2). Even the College of Rhode Island in Providence belonged to this provincial cluster, drawing as it did upon the farm families of southeastern Massachusetts and eastern Connecticut. Within fifty years the institutional setting of higher education in the region was transformed, creating what must have seemed like astonishing new options for the young men of New England.[5]

All the new colleges recruited students from the rural areas surrounding them. Through a series of specific economies, they attracted students whose families could not afford tuition or travel money and who had to stay near

TABLE 1 Mature Graduates at New England Colleges
(Aged 25 or Older)

	Harvard & Yale				New Colleges				All New England			
	Known Ages	Un-known	Mature No.	Mature %	Known Ages	Un-known	Mature No.	Mature %	Known Ages	Un-known	Mature No.	Mature %
1751-60	544	19	47	8.6	....	....	....	....	544	19	47	8.6
1761-70	709	37	74	10.4	9	3	2	22.2	718	40	76	10.6
1771-80	690	51	102	14.8	124	26	46	37.1	814	77	148	18.2
1781-90	744	49	101	13.6	249	26	86	34.5	993	75	187	18.8
1791-1800	693	13	101	14.6	571	79	176	30.8	1,264	92	277	21.9
1801-10	946	59	105	11.1	879	120	230	26.2	1,825	179	335	18.4
1811-20	1,036	178	87	8.4	1,104	108	325	29.4	2,140	286	412	19.3
1821-30	853	481	144	16.9	1,541	130	550	35.7	2,394	611	694	29.0
1831-40	1,260	114	191	15.2	2,013	141	682	33.9	3,273	255	873	26.7
1841-50	1,439	119	209	14.5	2,144	154	696	32.5	3,583	273	905	25.3
1851-60	1,837	39	218	11.9	2,656	91	885	33.3	4,493	130	1,103	24.5
1861-70*	231	1,864	18	7.8	2,272	232	723	31.8	4,599	....	959	20.9
1871-80*	259	2,520	24	9.3	2,469	458	667	27.0	5,706	....	1,048	18.4
1881-90*	378	3,224	50	13.2	2,498	807	635	25.4	6,907	....	1,314	19.0
1890-1900*	585	5,730	74	12.6	3,075	1,442	693	22.5	10,832	....	1,811	16.7

Sources: College biographical records, obituaries, class books, and faculty records.

Note: Figures for All New England include only the ten original colleges.

*Figures for Harvard and Yale, 1861-1900, are estimates based on one class per decade at each school. Figures for New Colleges are based on biographical registers, covering all colleges except Williams after 1865. Figures for All New England are estimates based on the known number of graduates, sample classes at Harvard and Yale, and more complete

TABLE 2   Founding of Provincial Colleges

	Year of First Degree
College of Rhode Island (Brown)	1769
Dartmouth College	1771
Williams College	1795
Middlebury College	1802
University of Vermont	1804
Bowdoin College	1806
Waterville College (Colby)	1822
Amherst College	1822

home to find work, food, and shelter. Provincial colleges devised calendars congenial to seasons of work in nearby fields and schools, and adopted inexpensive living arrangements. Most important, they made tuition cheap, almost a charity. By the time that Amherst was founded—the last of these institutions established before 1821—the college had actually come to be considered as a charitable institution.[6] In such a place a young man could cut costs; in 1827, when published catalogs made it easy for students to compare colleges, a young man at Amherst, Williams, or Brown could spend as little as half or two-thirds of the minimum amount spent by a student at Yale.[7]

Poor young men flooded these institutions. The whole student population increased from 200 to 2,700 between 1760 and 1860, and most of this growth took place, not at Harvard or Yale, but at the provincial colleges, where economies were greatest. By 1833, when Amherst and Waterville had firmly established themselves, the original ten colleges had 1,634 students—almost two-thirds of them in the eight new schools.[8] The provincial colleges, in a word, were functioning as institutions of mobility for the poor but promising village scholars of rural New England. They were one means by which a hard-pressed people sought to save some of its sons from failure in a declining rural social order that could not absorb them.

Fire and time have destroyed most documentary traces of the paupers in this student population, making it difficult to measure exactly their presence or determine the degree of their poverty. It is now impossible to count accurately the number of poor students—young men whose families may have given them some aid, but who had to find at least one additional source of support outside the family, either charity or self-help. Certainly not all the scholars at the new colleges were paupers, despite the systematic courting of very poor young men by Amherst and the other new institutions. Every college register listed students whose families must have paid all expenses. For the whole student population, the number of graduates over twenty-five years old probably represents a minimum indicator of the number of students from families too poor to pay the costs of higher education—at least one-fourth of all New England students between 1800 and 1860.[9] At some point in the decades between 1791 and 1830, when the number of mature graduates per decade climbed from 277 to 694 (see Table 1), the number of poor and mature students appears to have reached a critical level, when the pure power of their absolute numbers

—as distinct from their percentage in the student population—began to force changes in charity and in higher education.

At individual institutions the number of poor students certainly exceeded one-fourth the student body. In the case of Amherst College (where fire destroyed financial records in 1838) about 500 of the first 1,300 students relied on college-controlled charity funds between 1821 and 1845, for which they had to document some degree of poverty.[10] At Bowdoin College in 1829 and 1830, a rare combination of complete lists of its schoolkeepers and charity students has survived, making it possible to analyze the entire student body of this institution for these years in terms of student income. More than half of Bowdoin's 114 students in 1829 were poor—sixty-four of them had to teach school or apply for charity funds to cover tuition and other expenses. The list of schoolkeepers shows that about one-third (forty-five students) kept school to help support themselves. The list of students who received grants from college-administered tuition funds also contains the names of about one-third (forty-three students) of the Bowdoin enrollment. These students had to produce documentary evidence of poverty before they could receive grants. A third list shows that six students received aid from the American Education Society, a Boston institution organized in 1815 to help indigent young men prepare for the ministry. The names of twenty-eight students—about one-fourth of those enrolled—appeared more than once on the Bowdoin poverty lists; these students must have been totally indigent in the sense that they received no material support from their families, but relied solely upon charity funds, tuition grants, and their own income from teaching. In the early nineteenth century, these sources together could have supported a student who was on his own and without family aid.[11] And what was happening at Bowdoin was happening at the other provincial colleges, too.[12]

Only the poorest of paupers—the indigent beneficiaries of the national education societies—can be identified precisely for all of New England. All of them had to provide evidence that they were poor. Education societies, appearing after 1810, required their beneficiaries to prove that they were destitute. In 1810-11, none of these indigents existed; in 1830-31, they numbered 193 at nine New England colleges, or 13 percent of the region's 1,462 college students. Before 1840 they exceeded 15 percent.[13] "Infiltration" really fails as a metaphor to describe the sudden appearance of these indigents between 1815 and 1830. Given the scale of higher education in the early nineteenth century, their coming constituted an invasion, a sudden presence to be rationalized somehow and managed by the colleges.

The movement of poor young men into the student population resulted from the same social changes that caused a simultaneous exodus of young people from rural New England in the generation after the American Revolution. The same crowding onto marginal farmlands that caused the massive emigration to the West and to new industrial cities between 1790 and 1860 produced this comparatively smaller movement into New England colleges. Sons were abandoning farms in rural and hill communities where population was pressing on the supply of good land. For almost a century before 1800, the density of agricultural population had been increasing constantly throughout New England. Eastern Massachusetts and the Connecticut River Valley had already been densely settled by the early eighteenth century. After 1713 new settlers filled the rough terrain of Worcester County and moved beyond the valley into the hills of what are now Hampshire, Franklin, Hampden, and Berkshire counties, where towns were settled between 1720 and 1750. Then even the less desirable lands, which had been ignored for a century, began to fill with inhabitants, prefiguring the crowding which would come by the end of the eighteenth century. By 1770 the best of southern New England had been claimed and settled; and Maine, New Hampshire, Vermont, and the hill towns of western Massachusetts were filling with settlers. Throughout New England between the eve of the Revolution and 1800, young men trying to establish farms increasingly had to take poorer and smaller tracts of land and seek income from sources other than their small-scale farming.[14]

The mountain towns of western Massachusetts (which provided Williams College and Amherst College with most of their first students) experienced this cycle of growth, crowding, and exodus between 1770 and 1830. Between 1770 and 1790, the towns lying entirely or partially in the hills of Hampshire, Hampden, and Franklin counties had become thickly settled; some of them contained four times as many people in 1800 as they would in 1900, after a long process of abandonment. All twenty-five towns above the 500-foot contour in these three counties lost population between 1800 and 1860. Another twenty towns straddling the 500-foot contour between the hills and the lowlands of the Connecticut River Valley lost population during the first four decades of the nineteenth century—before reviving slightly. Only five agricultural towns in the three counties gained in population, and all of them were on the river itself, near the twenty-two towns that were growing because of industrialization.[15]

The difficult farm life in these rural communities pushed the young and the poor from New England out onto new lands in New York, Pennsylvania, and Ohio. Desertion of the Hampshire and Berkshire hill towns appears to have occurred in two phases. From the Revolution until 1840, migration from the uplands was caused by poor soil and the difficulty of farming rough terrain. After 1840 the railroad, in addition to the land factors, further diminished the population in these towns by bringing cheaper farm products from the West into eastern markets. In this way, farming became economically a more hazardous vocation for young men in hilly New England towns which were also unsuitable for manufacturing.[16]

Young men born in this area between 1790 and 1840 were confronted by depressing alternatives. Some could stay on their fathers' farms, but fewer than in the preceding generation. Only a very few could remain in their homes by working as hired hands. Most of them simply had to get out, and the majority went either to other lands or—especially after 1820—to the cities, where they became workers and clerks. After 1820, the younger generation fled the farms *en masse*, and among the deserters were those who went down to Amherst or over to Williamstown to join the new colleges and prepare for the professional lives that would take them away forever.[17]

It was from families in the hills of western Massachusetts, with their surplus sons, that Amherst and Williams drew heavily for their students before 1860. Between 1820 and 1860, Amherst graduated 306 students from Hampden, Hampshire, and Franklin counties; more than half of these—160 in all—came from the forty-seven towns that were experiencing the exodus. Another 162 graduates had come to Amherst from similar towns in Worcester County, just to the east. Between 1795 and 1860 Williams College graduated 323 students from the three counties straddling the Connecticut River; 218 of these, or 67 percent, came from the same declining towns. More than half the students coming to Amherst and Williams from these three counties came from the poor and declining hill towns.[18]

One of these communities was Southampton, Massachusetts, which stretches westward from lowlands near the Connecticut River into the hills of Hampshire County. The length of the journey from Southampton to Amherst, twenty miles northeast, made daily commuting impossible. Williamstown was a hard day's ride through the mountains. Yet, between 1795 and 1860, Southampton produced a large number of students, as did the cluster of surrounding towns. To the colleges at Amherst and Williamstown, Southampton sent more young men than any other town in Hampshire, Franklin, or Hampden counties with the exception of the town of Amherst itself.[19] In the local history of Southampton, it is possible to see the social changes working in all these communities and to analyze the origins of its students, as well as the common motives that were propelling young men from the town.[20]

By 1800 Southampton had already become a mature settlement, with about as many persons as it would contain a century later. It had been settled between 1730 and 1741 by Northampton residents, predominantly young men who had been crowded out of the old settlement. Within three generations, Southampton itself had become crowded, farms being taken not only in its western lowlands but also on stony hills to the east in an area known as Fomer, abundantly settled in the early nineteenth century and finally abandoned by 1900. Through the first half of the nineteenth century, almost all the seventy-two towns in the three counties were about the size of Southampton; as late as 1840, only five of them had populations exceeding 3,000 people. In 1830 Southampton reached its population peak of 1,244, a total it could not equal in 1930. Between 1800 and 1830, males of twenty and thirty years were outnumbered by females of their age cohort in the town, mainly because of male emigration to the West. Southampton also began to send some of its young men to college.[21]

In all the eighteenth century, only two Southampton boys had graduated from college: Jonathan Judd, Jr. (Yale, 1765), son of the first minister; and David Searl (Dartmouth, 1784), the town's first impoverished scholar. Searl was an orphan whose father died intestate, leaving a divided estate; Searl had fought in the Revolution, and then he went to Dartmouth, the nearest college, where he graduated at age twenty-nine. Then he disappeared into the West, where he probably became another Yankee schoolkeeper among the thousands of other New England Ichabods.[22]

Southampton produced a surge of students between 1801 and 1840, the years of heaviest emigration, while the student population of New England

TABLE 3   Students from Southampton, 1761-1860

Graduating Classes	Number of Students
1761-1800	2
1801-1810	8
1811-1820	11
1821-1830	10
1831-1840	15
1841-1850	2
1851-1860	2
Total	50

Note: These figures include both graduates and nongraduates of each graduating class.

was doubling. Until the pressures favoring emigration subsided after 1840, Southampton contributed a regular number of students every decade (see Table 3). Altogether, at least fifty young men left Southampton between 1761 and 1860 to join the student population.[23] Most of them departed between 1801 and 1840.[24] The reasons for their departures and for the sudden surge in student numbers in the early nineteenth century can be inferred from their experiences in the town, their family histories, and their student careers.

All Southampton's students between 1801 and 1840 experienced the revivals of religion, local manifestations of the Second Great Awakening, that struck the town during this period. There can be no doubt that the motives that inspired local boys to seek higher education were related to these revivals and to the influence of the town's second minister, the Reverend Vinson Gould. Gould came to Southampton in 1801 and remained as pastor until 1832. His predecessor, Jonathan Judd, Sr., had witnessed many revivals during his long tenure, beginning in the days of Jonathan Edwards. But Judd saw no revivals to compare with Gould's, nor had he launched a procession of young scholars like those whom Gould sent to Williams and Amherst. Gould worked hard among the town's youth, seeking out the most promising young men to advance toward the ministry. The lives of almost all Southampton's students intersected with the activities of Vinson Gould: he encouraged them to study, he found financial aid for them, or he instructed them himself. Ministers poured from Southampton during his years there. Judd's ministry of sixty years had yielded none; Gould's three decades produced thirty-six.[25] The revivals did not exactly generate a local intellectual renaissance or produce a sudden, romantic yearning for knowledge among the town's youth. They did, however, create considerable interest in ministerial careers.

In this respect, Southampton merely experienced the same phenomenon that contemporaries were noting in other New England towns. "Country churches among the hills produce more ministers in proportion to their numbers than churches in large cities," observed directors of the American Education Society in 1867. The most abundant sources were the hill towns, they noted.

TABLE 4   Birth Order of Southampton Students, 1761-1860

Order of sons	1st	2nd	3rd	4th	?
Number of students	14	18	8	8	2

Note: The years covered by this table refer to graduating classes, not to years of birth. This will be true of all tables on Southampton students. These figures include only those brothers alive in the year of each student's graduation.

No wise man would think of going down to Cape Cod, if he wanted to start up a large number of new candidates for the ministry. He would find the young men there all pre-occupied. They are all ambitious to become mates or masters of vessels. But if one desired to secure young men for this purpose, he would go rather to the mountain towns in Franklin, Hampshire and Berkshire counties, or to New Hampshire and Vermont.[26]

Under the impact of the revivals and Mr. Gould, Southampton became a nursery for the nineteenth-century ministry, as did other towns in the hills. Yet Gould was working in a field prepared by other, more material causes.

Southampton's students would have faced a landless existence had they elected to stay home.[27] Thus, while they may all have been drawn to college by piety or passion for learning, the fact remains that most of them, as younger brothers among older siblings, as members of large families, as inheritors of their fathers' meager estates, would have been driven from the town in any case by material necessity. And in fact, most of them were younger sons in a town where family custom once again favored eldest sons with the largest pieces of inheritable land, if they wanted it (see Table 4). Only fourteen first sons appeared among Southampton students, and, of these, only eight might have inherited sufficient land or property to have settled in Southampton. The rest of the students—thirty-six—confronted the classic difficulties of younger sons in a crowded rural society.

They came, moreover, from families with large numbers of sons—brothers who might share in any divided estates (see Table 5). More than half of them had two or more brothers alive when their classes graduated from college. They came from mature families with full complements of children, most of whom either still depended on the family or might share in its estate (see Table 6). More than half came from families with at least six children surviving at the time of the student's graduation. In these respects, the situation of Southampton students was similar to that of countless other young men from large families in the region, at a time when rural New Englanders were just beginning to discover contraception as a method of limiting family size, preventing poverty, and controlling the glut of young men.[28]

These young men who presented themselves at the colleges of New England shared a set of difficulties common to most young men in the region. As a

TABLE 5   Brothers of Southampton Students, 1761-1860

Number of brothers	0	1	2	3	4	5	?
Number of students	3	13	13	13	5	1	2

Note: These figures include only those brothers alive in the year of each student's graduation.

TABLE 6   Size of Families Producing Southampton Students, 1761-1860

Children in Family	1	2	3	4	5	6	7	8	9	10	?
Number of Students	0	0	4	7	7	8	8	4	6	4	2

Note: These figures include only those children alive in the year of each student's graduation.

group, the fifty students from Southampton who went to college in the century between 1761 (when Jonathan Judd, Jr., went off to Yale) and 1860 had very limited opportunities available to them at home. Southampton simply could not contain them.

They were impelled by negative motives. If they remained in town as farm laborers, the one local pursuit left to them, they faced a new state of dependence on other men, who might control their lives and labor. The diary of Bela Bates Edwards (Amherst, 1824), the only Southampton student who left a literary record of his youth, describes how he was driven from the town. Edwards was his father's second son. Knowing—as many New England families know—that only one son could stay home, his family had planned for years to tithe him to the ministry, giving him an option. Bela resisted leaving Southampton, and he hesitated before joining the ministry, as his diary reveals: he acquiesced reluctantly. Comparable literary sources by students from other towns reveal a similar, negative frame of mind, a sense of bleak expectations.[29]

In this, the students cannot have differed from other young men leaving rural New England. The question of why some young men chose college, while most did not, must unfortunately be answered less with evidence than with logic. Sheer chance and disposition probably determined the choice for most individuals. Significantly, no rigid rule determined that students be taken from the sickly, from among oldest or youngest sons, or only from families above a certain economic and social level. Almost anyone might conceivably have decided to become a student.

Ultimately, two factors determined who went to college and who did not: the vocational structure of the early nineteenth century (which held forth certain opportunities to specific people) and the idiosyncrasies of personal history. Professional prospects for young men like those from Southampton lay primarily in the ministry and in teaching, the two vocations attracting almost all the town's graduates. In a community like this, young men could begin to prepare for the ministry more readily than for law or medicine because the town's professional connections were limited almost exclusively to the ministry—and because there were funds to support ministerial students. For teaching, young men virtually prepared themselves; and teachers could support themselves while going to college or looking for a permanent profession outside the ministry. No youths who lacked piety or intellectual "parts," as they said, would have had much opportunity or interest in either of these vocations, or in college.

On the other hand, those who did evince religious sensibilities or the demeanor of Hawthorne's schoolmasters had both the chances and the motives. It was they who might attract the attention of the only man in town who still had any general control over these decisions: the minister, the man who could ease the way to Amherst by helping boys to prepare or by finding money. And it was they who had to have a college education. In preaching and teaching, success required at least some years at college.

There would be no great material reward in these callings, but through them a young man might gain, in a highly mobile age, a modicum of control over his own geographical mobility. These callings might let him settle down, either at home or near home; in New England perhaps, and at a higher station than that of a hired hand. They would spare him the uncertainties of joining the farmer-emigrants in the West or the clerks and laborers of the cities. At the same time, they might also help him preserve some of the personal independence that families like his had known for generations and extend the hope, at least, of some control over his own life and labor.

Intelligence and intellectual curiosity, family size and overcrowding on the farm, the minister, the revivals, and piety—whichever of these influences and motives may have operated in individual cases, all of them now came together in ways that made the colleges attractive places to a growing number of poor young men.

Of the fifty Southampton students, only seven had social origins that suggest that necessity need not have propelled them from the community. The family estates of these seven ranked in the upper 5 percent of the town's tax lists; either their families held blocks of land ranging from 250 to 600 acres (the largest in town) or their fathers were among the town's few professionals. Two students were the sons of ministers, one the son of a doctor. Only one of the seven students might have had trouble paying college bills. They depended entirely on their families, who could easily have afforded to pay all expenses. Their estates, while modest compared to some in Northampton, were substantial enough to cover minimum costs of four years at college, or about $500 between 1800 and 1840. Wherever evidence is available on the family estates of these seven students, it indicates a range of $4,000 to $12,000, or roughly ten times the cost of higher education for one son as a minimum base of financial resources. With one exception, these most affluent students started college before they were twenty-one and finished in their very early twenties, indicating easy, uninterrupted student careers. (Only Henry L. Edwards [Amherst, 1847] was relatively mature, graduating at twenty-six; and his father paid all his college bills in cash.[30] Edwards's late start may be explained by a late religious conversion and a tardy decision to study for the ministry.) Southampton's wealthiest families, moreover, were the only ones with any sort of tradition of higher education: two fathers in the group had graduated from college.

Yet, even among these seven students in easy circumstances, necessity was working. Isaac Parsons, Jr. (Yale, 1811), was born to the wealthiest family in western Southampton. But even in his case, elements of necessity had helped to prompt his departure from the family farm for Yale and a subsequent career in the ministry. He was the second of two sons and the last of six children. His brother Theodore, nine years his senior, was in line to inherit the farm, which he did in 1819. In 1821, the year of the first itemized tax assessment in Southampton, the Parsons estate included 438 acres, three horses, two oxen, six cows, assorted younger cattle, swine, and some of Southampton's few carriages. While Isaac, Jr., might have shared in this bounty, his only real portion came in the form of higher education at Yale. His father paid all the bills; young Isaac graduated at twenty-one.[31]

For the forty-three Southampton students who were either orphans or who came from families below the wealthiest 5 percent on the tax lists, necessity was more grim. Their families owned smaller plots of land, ranging downward from 230 acres, the majority holding between 50 and 200 acres,[32] though some had no land whatever. They undertook higher education with less certainty and pursued it more precariously than Isaac Parsons, Jr., having to help support themselves, and were at graduation older than their more wealthy neighbors. They ranged from age twenty to thirty-two at graduation, with more than half finishing at twenty-five or older.

As many as twenty-eight of these poorer students may have received significant aid from their families in paying college bills, but this meant sacrifice. For families below the wealthiest 5 percent in Southampton, financing a son's higher education was very difficult. Instead of simply giving their sons $100 or $200 to cover the minimum expenses of a year at college, the fathers of these young men charged these amounts as "advances" against their sons' portions of the family estates; the advances were then deducted in the wills. At least thirteen students from such families received such advances, in amounts varying from full payment of college costs to mere gifts of clothing. Bela Bates Edwards probably relied entirely on his father, who owned 175 acres and was in the top 10 percent on the tax lists. Still, when Edwards's father drew up his will in 1826, he left most of his estate to his wife and his first son, Elisha; to his second son, Bela, he gave some money, "in addition to what I have expended in giving him a public education." With his father's aid, Bela Bates Edwards finished his studies at twenty-two, but this had required determination and foresight. Despite Bela's reluctance to leave Southampton and his occasional walks home—he was overcome by homesickness—his family's determination prevailed. Their financial arrangements also succeeded, and Bela Bates Edwards, having finished his studies at Amherst, never again lived in Southampton.[33]

In the cases of Alvan Chapman (Amherst, 1830) and his brother Mahlon (Amherst, 1832), family assistance was on a smaller scale. Their father's will suggests that both sons may have received advances. But Chapman was a shoemaker with an estate assessed at only $525 in 1830. He may have clothed his sons and given them small sums of spending money, but he cannot have supported both of them at once at Amherst, for expenditures of more than $200 a year would have consumed his estate. His sons must have sought other sources of funds as well, a possible one being a wealthy Southampton farmer named Silas Sheldon, who had no children and who apparently loaned money to students preparing for the ministry.[34]

At least five students, and perhaps six, derived significant support from the estates of deceased fathers, though only one could have received enough inheritance money to put himself through college; but even in these cases sacrifice was demanded, since the young men were giving up their chances to own a little land in order to pay for an education. In addition to the thirteen who received advances and the five or six who could have used portions of estates, nine other Southampton students may have received some family aid, but if so they left no record of their arrangements.

The remaining fifteen students from Southampton all relied on charity. In terms of collegiate society, they were the indigent poor who could expect nothing, or practically nothing, from family sources. Only three of the charity students may have received even an occasional small gift or loan. Eight of them were orphans. Like the rest of Southampton's pauper-scholars, the fifteen indigents kept school, delayed their matriculation, and graduated at advanced ages (see Table 7). Only four charity scholars from Southampton graduated at twenty-four or younger; eleven were twenty-five or older. They appeared among Southampton's students after 1817, during the ascendance of the new education societies, upon which they relied heavily. Altogether, one-third of Southampton's students between 1800 and 1860 submitted documentary proof that they were indigent.

The indigents came from a broad section of Southampton society. Their families often lived in respectable circumstances, worked hard on their farms, but confronted the prospect of having partially dependent sons unable to maintain themselves. Some indigents, it is true, were drawn from among the town's orphans and dependent families; but they were not drawn exclusively from beggars, the poor farm, or the almshouse, either in Southampton or in New England at large.

The father of Jeremiah Pomeroy (Amherst, 1829) owned 182 acres on the western slope of Pomeroy's Mountain, not far from Isaac Parsons's farm. Necessity began to work in Jeremiah's life from the moment of his birth in 1804. He was the third of four surviving sons and seven surviving children when he graduated. Evidently, he had determined for himself to give up any claim to a small portion of the farm in favor of education at Amherst; he may have received some help from home, since his father left him only a token twenty dollars in the will. An older brother, Wells, originally received

TABLE 7   Graduation Ages of Southampton Students, 1761-1860

Ages	20	21	22	23	24	25	26	27	28	29	30	31	32
Family-supported	2	2	1	0	1	0	1						
Family-aided	1	3	3	1	8	4	3	1	1	2	0	0	1
Charity-aided	0	2	0	1	1	4	0	2	0	2	3		
Total students	3	7	4	2	10	8	4	3	1	4	3	0	1

Note: These figures include ages for three nongraduates and forty-seven graduates. For nongraduates, the "graduation age" was based on the age at which a student entered college and assumed a four-year course. "Family-supported" refers to students whose families probably gave full support. "Family-aided" refers to students who received aid from their families, but not as free grants or in sums sufficient for full support. "Charity-aided" refers to students who drew upon various charity funds.

most of the estate; then the youngest, Cornelius, took over the farm after living with his aging parents. Two other brothers chose to leave the homestead. There were simply too many sons for 182 mountain acres.[35]

Jeremiah Pomeroy was absent from college for long periods in 1826 and 1827, probably keeping school. He first applied for aid from the Hampshire Education Society in 1823, when Reverend Gould spoke in his behalf. In 1825, when he entered Amherst College, he became a full beneficiary of the H.E.S., a local charitable society formed in 1815 that eventually aided seven Southampton students. Later, Pomeroy also became a beneficiary of the American Education Society. In accepting this aid, he again declared himself indigent, and Vinson Gould again testified to the truth of his declaration.[36]

What is significant about Pomeroy is that his was one of the two highest-ranking families in Southampton to produce a charity student. In 1821 his father's estate ranked among the top 15 percent on the tax lists and his family among the top twenty-seven property-owning families in town. The father's economic position did not change significantly before his death in 1845. And Pomeroy could not plead the hardship of an orphan when he applied for charity. His father owned two horses, four oxen, four cows, and a number of lesser farm animals but no carriages and only a small house with a south room, "kitchin," a finished bedroom, another bedroom, buttery, cellar, and washroom. Theoretically, any student from a family ranking below the Pomeroys could have qualified for aid as an indigent. In Southampton perhaps thirty-three students fell below Jeremiah Pomeroy in terms of family wealth. Jeremiah Pomeroy was the wealthiest indigent in town, and his status as a beneficiary indicates just how high in the scale of local society it was now possible to stand and yet be considered "poor."[37]

Erastus Clapp, on the other hand, came from the lower extreme. Clapp was born in 1792 and was orphaned in 1809, when his father's estate was declared "insolvent." At one time the Clapp homestead had encompassed about 200 acres near White Loaf Mountain, in the western part of town; by 1809, when Erastus Clapp was seventeen, it was all gone. Clapp earned a reputation for depending "almost wholly" on his own exertions in financing his education. Actually, he and his brother Reuben, born in 1789, both relied heavily on charity. Reuben became a beneficiary of the Connecticut Education Society sometime in 1814 or 1815, but died while still a student at Yale. Erastus was the second of four sons, the fifth of eight children surviving when his father died. He became a beneficiary of the Hampshire Education Society in 1817 (when Pastor Gould was serving as a society director). Clapp received at least sixty-five dollars from the society between 1817 and 1819 while studying at Williams—enough to cover one-fourth of his expenses. The rest he must have earned himself, as local tradition had it. He was twenty-six before he even started to college, and he graduated from Union College in 1822, at age thirty, having experienced delays typical for these poorest students.[38]

Southampton's first fifty students could not afford college life in high style—or, on their own, in any style at all. Their poverty revealed itself even in their choices of institutions; they chose the cheapest. It was not until Williams was founded that significant numbers of Southampton boys went to college, and then almost all of them went there because it was nearby and inexpensive. When Amherst opened in 1821, just twenty miles away, they abandoned Williams altogether for the new institution, founded as a charity school. Only two went to Harvard (with self-help and charity) and eight to Yale (three of them on charity funds). Williams and Amherst, so decisively the choices of this town's youth, had opened new options at a difficult time.

Towns all over New England began to produce students from families like those in Southampton in the early nineteenth century. Hundreds of students of similar social origins enrolled at the colleges with momentous consequences for themselves, for the colleges as institutions, and even for the society into which they were graduated. They overwhelmed traditional sources of aid for students. Less dependent on the family or the college, they created a new style of student life, with greater independence, maturity, and commerce between students and the adult society. They brought to student society a new variety, a mixing of ages and classes. In time, they would demolish the old form of collegiate community. In time, too, they would precipitate a crisis in governing the student population, as the community arrangements that once ordered the behavior and intellectual activity of students disappeared. They altered student life for everyone in collegiate institutions, but especially for the poor.

Notes

1 All expressions associated with poverty here are defined exclusively in terms of the student population. It was possible, therefore, for a student not remarkably poor in the context of his community to have been quite poor educationally, in the context of a college. "Poor" and "pauper" refer to all students who received essential support from sources outside the family. "Indigent" denotes those students who were destitute—totally dependent on sources outside the family—or who received funds from charity; in the early nineteenth century this was the meaning of the term with reference to students. In using these terms, I have come close to adopting the way in which Horace Mann defined poverty: ". . . Every man is POOR, in an educational sense, who cannot both spare and equip his children for school for the entire period." (Mann's entire period was ten months each year between ages four and sixteen.) See Mann, "Report for 1847," in *Life and Works of Horace Mann* (Boston: Lee and Shepard, 1891), 4:201-02. See also Paul Mann, "The Social Status of Oxford Undergraduates, 1660-1685" (Paper delivered at the Davis Center for Historical Studies, Princeton University, March 2, 1973), p. 5.

2 Graduating classes at colonial Harvard and Yale did include a wide range of ages but contained large clusters of graduates between nineteen and twenty-one, all of whom started to college before reaching maturity (see Appendix A).

3 These statements are based on analysis of the ages of all graduates listed in the published biographical registers and other records of the ten New England colleges that granted degrees before 1825—Harvard, Yale, Brown, Dartmouth, Williams, Middlebury, Vermont, Bowdoin, Waterville (Colby), and Amherst. Ages were determined in years and months, then rounded off to the nearest year. In order to keep ages comparable for the eighteenth and nineteenth centuries, September was assumed to be the month of graduation for all students. See also W. Scott Thomas, "Changes in the Age of College Graduation," *Popular Science Monthly* 63 (1903): 159-71.

4 Student records for the early nineteenth century show that the older members of graduating classes were consistently the poorest. One minimal way to document this relationship between maturity and poverty is to compare the ages of students who received charity with the ages of all other students—many of whom were also poor and mature but whose names did not appear on charity lists. In the first twenty-one classes at Amherst College between 1822 and 1842, it is possible to identify 213 graduates who received charity from the American Education Society; they represented 29 percent of the 729 graduates in these years. Ages can be determined for 211 beneficiaries and for 505 other graduates, accounting for 716 graduates in all. Seventy percent of the A.E.S. beneficiaries graduated at twenty-five or older, compared to 31 percent of those students not appearing on A.E.S. lists. A large majority of graduates aged twenty-seven or older were A.E.S. beneficiaries, and the most mature members of each class were nearly always charity students. Their average age at graduation was twenty-six, compared to twenty-three for other students. (For detailed figures, see Table 13.) Sources for this information are William L. Montague, ed., *Biographical Record of the Alumni of Amherst College, During Its First Half Century, 1821-1871* (Amherst, Mass.: J. E. Williams, 1883), pp. 9-194; and Beneficiary Account Book, American Education Society Archives, Congregational Library, Boston, Mass.

Philippe Aries discusses the social significance of the age structure of student populations, together with comparative trends in European schools, in *Centuries of Childhood: A Social History of Family Life*, trans. Robert Baldick (New York: Alfred A. Knopf, 1962), pp. 189-240.

5 Donald Tewksbury, *The Founding of American Colleges and Universities Before the Civil War* (New York: Teachers College, Columbia University, 1932), pp. 32-38. Tewksbury dated Amherst by its charter year, 1825; actually, Amherst began instruction in 1821 and graduated its first class in 1822. Washington College (now Trinity) in Hartford was chartered in 1823 and granted its first degrees in 1827. My study omits students at the five New England institutions founded between 1823 and 1860—Trinity (1823), Wesleyan (1831), Norwich (1834), Holy Cross (1843), and Tufts (1852). I confined my study to the first ten colleges primarily because I could obtain source material that was comparable in character for the entire group of original institutions. I am convinced, after additional research, that including the five newer institutions would have altered my generalizations in no significant way.

6 The first page of the 1822 Amherst College catalog advertised a $50,000 charity fund for the indigent and pious; see also William S. Tyler, *History of Amherst College Dur-*

ing Its First Half Century, 1821-1871 (Springfield, Mass.: Clark W. Bryan and Company, 1873), pp. 40-50.

7 See the printed catalogs for 1827 and 1828 of Williams, Amherst, Brown, and Yale.

8 Arthur M. Comey, "The Growth of New England Colleges," *Educational Review* 1 (1891): 211; "View of the American Colleges, 1833," *American Quarterly Register* 5 (1833): 332-33.

9 This is a minimum estimate, since it includes only those students who delayed higher education until they had become adults of twenty-one or older. With only rare exceptions, these mature students were poor; moreover, there were large numbers of the poor among younger students, who are not counted in this estimate.

10 Heman Humphrey, *Valedictory Address, Delivered at Amherst College* (Amherst, Mass.: J. S. & C. Adams, 1845), pp. 16-17. Humphrey was counting only those students who received aid from the college charity fund. His estimate did not include beneficiaries of the American Education Society, though many students received aid from both sources. Humphrey placed the whole number of college-fund beneficiaries at 501, including both graduates and nongraduates, between 1821 and 1845. By 1845 Amherst had graduated 810 and had enrolled about 555 nongraduates, by my count—a total of 1,365 students. Humphrey was using his own recollection, since records of the college charity fund before 1838 were destroyed by fire.

11 "Record of proceedings of Committee on applications for benefit of grant by General Court of Massachusetts to Bowdoin College," February 12, 1830, and June 5, 1830, Bowdoin College Special Collections, Brunswick, Me.; "Record of Executive Government, 1825-1848," Fall 1829 and November 1830, Bowdoin Collections; "A.E.S. Records & Monthly Concert, Bowdoin College," list of names following the constitution, Bowdoin Collections.

12 Compared to the seven other new colleges, Bowdoin appears to have enrolled slightly fewer beneficiaries of the education societies in 1829-30, a few more of its own charity students, and about the same number of schoolkeepers. Precise comparisons between all colleges cannot be drawn, since the records of individual institutions vary and are incomplete. Records of many charity disbursements have disappeared, and the names of schoolkeepers were not kept with regularity or precision at every institution. For general comparisons on the number of charity students in the early 1830s, however, see "View of the American Colleges, 1831," *American Quarterly Register* 3 (1831): 294-95; and on the prevalence of schoolkeeping, see Elias Cor-

nelius to Francis Wayland, January 18, 1830, Letter Book 1, A.E.S. Archives.

13 "American Colleges, 1831," pp. 294-95; "American Colleges, 1833," pp. 332-33.

14 There is a large literature on crowding and poverty in New England during the period between the Revolution and the Civil War. See Lois Kimball Mathews, *The Expansion of New England* (1909; reprint ed., New York: Russell & Russell, Inc., 1962); Percy W. Bidwell, "The Agricultural Revolution in New England," *American Historical Review* 26 (1921): 683-702; Bidwell, "Population Growth in Southern New England, 1810-1860," *Quarterly Publications of the American Statistical Association*, n.s. 15 (1917): 813-39; Bidwell, "Rural Economy in New England at the Beginning of the Nineteenth Century," *Transactions of the Connecticut Academy of Arts and Sciences* 20 (1916): 241-399. Bidwell described an area of poverty throughout inland New England that most travelers did not observe because their itineraries took them through prosperous sections; see especially his "Rural Economy," pp. 368-74, 383-91. Kenneth Lockridge has focused upon the revolutionary implications of crowding and poverty in "Land, Population and the Evolution of New England Society, 1630-1790," *Past and Present*, no. 39 (1968), pp. 62-80. See also Lockridge, *A New England Town: The First Hundred Years* (New York: W. W. Norton & Company, 1970), pp. 181-86; Harold Fisher Wilson, *The Hill Country of Northern New England* (New York: Columbia University Press, 1936); Lewis D. Stilwell, *Migration from Vermont*, Proceedings of the Vermont Historical Society (Montpelier, Vt., 1937) 5: 63-245; and Daniel H. Calhoun, *Professional Lives in America* (Cambridge, Mass.: Harvard University Press, 1965), pp. 160-62.

15 Lester Earl Klimm, *The Relation Between Certain Population Changes and the Physical Environment in Hampden, Hampshire, and Franklin Counties, Massachusetts, 1790-1925* (Philadelphia: University of Pennsylvania, 1933), pp. 5-10, 41-67, 106-09.

16 Ibid., pp. 47-48.

17 Bidwell, "Agricultural Revolution," pp. 700-01. Young men who found their way into the student population certainly accounted for only a small fraction of this emigration, and the numbers who went from farm to college were too small to suggest that this form of social mobility was common or easy in the early nineteenth century. These students were not significant in this way but rather in terms of their impact upon New England colleges. For a study that does address the social mobility of Harvard and Yale students, see P. M. G. Har-

ris, "The Social Origins of American Leaders: The Demographic Foundations," *Perspectives in American History* 3 (1969): 159-344.

18 These figures are based on counts of the residences of all graduates of Amherst and Williams before 1860, listed in Montague, *Biographical Record of Amherst*, and Calvin Durfee, *Williams Biographical Annals* (Boston: Lee and Shepard, 1871). See also Beverly McAnear, "The Selection of an Alma Mater by Pre-Revolutionary Students," *Pennsylvania Magazine of History and Biography* 73 (1949): 429-40.

During the 1840s, when only 52.5 percent of all Massachusetts residents lived in towns of under 3,000 people, Amherst and Williams were drawing 80.2 percent of their Massachusetts students from towns this small. Conversely, 22.2 percent of the whole population lived in six cities of over 10,000 inhabitants, but only 5.8 percent of the Massachusetts students attending Amherst and Williams came from these cities. In the early nineteenth century Harvard drew the vast majority of its students from eastern Massachusetts; it was exceptional in the urban composition of its student body. In the 1840s, 54.8 percent of its Massachusetts students came from the six large cities (most of them from Boston), and only 5.0 percent came from communities of under 3,000 persons. Yale drew heavily from rural Connecticut and relied upon New Haven to a lesser degree than Harvard did upon Boston. Northern New England colleges drew predictably large percentages—80 percent and above—from communities of under 3,000 people. Sources for these figures are U.S. Census, *Compendium of the Enumeration of the Inhabitants and Statistics of the United States* (Washington, D.C.: Thomas Allen, 1841), pp. 4-19, and college catalogs, which listed places of residence.

19 The five towns in Hampshire, Hampden, and Franklin counties with the largest numbers of graduates from Amherst and Williams were as follows: Amherst, 51; Southampton, 33; Northampton, 32; Westhampton, 28; and Hadley, 25. These figures, too, are based on counts of residences of all graduates listed in Montague, *Biographical Record of Amherst*, and Durfee, *Williams Biographical Annals*.

20 In analyzing the origins of students, historians have relied on matriculation books and biographical registers in college and university archives. Scholars working with the student populations of English universities have used such materials almost exclusively, assuming, with some justification, that the status categories given in these records were comparatively precise. In dealing with motives, they have used similar

sources, making logical inferences from aggregate biographical data. For New England before the 1870s, no documentation in college archives and nothing in the voluminous biographical registers (which stress later careers) provides adequate evidence on the origins or social status of students. To gather this kind of information, students simply must be traced from the colleges back to the towns they left, and to their families of origin. Ultimately, local historical records and some methods of demographic history offer the only ways to answer questions of origin and, perhaps, of motive.

21 Bela Bates Edwards, *Address Delivered at Southampton, Mass., at the Centennial Celebration* (Andover, Mass.: Allen, Morrill and Wardwell, 1841), pp. 10-11; Wendell Hubbard Bash, "Factors Influencing Family and Community Organization in a New England Town, 1730 to 1940: A Study of Southampton, Massachusetts" (Ph.D. diss., Harvard University, 1941), pp. 30-31, 34, 126-33, 148-54.

22 George T. Chapman, ed., *Sketches of the Alumni of Dartmouth College* (Cambridge, Mass.: Riverside Press, 1867), p. 35; Sardis Chapman, "The Chapman Manuscript" [Genealogical and historical records of the town of Southampton, Mass.], 2 vols., Manuscript, Forbes Library, Northampton, Mass., n.d., 2:271; distribution of estate of Josiah Searl, December 14, 1779, Box 128, no. 38, Probate Registry, Hall of Records, Northampton, Mass.

23 This figure is based on my own findings in the biographical registers of New England colleges and in genealogies and histories of Southampton families. Lists of Southampton students appear in at least five sources: Edwards, *Address at Southampton*, pp. 49-50; Bash, "Factors Influencing Family and Community," p. 58; John P. Richardson, *Sketches of Southampton's Sons in the Ministry* (New Haven: Hoggson & Robinson, 1891); W. B. Gay, comp., *Gazeteer of Hampshire County, Mass., 1654-1887* (Syracuse, N.Y.: W. B. Gay & Co., n.d.), p. 420; and *History of the Connecticut Valley in Massachusetts*, 2 vols. (Philadelphia: Louis H. Everts, 1879), 1:307-08. I have eliminated some names from these lists and added a few not found in them. (For a complete list, see Tables 14-18.) I have included both graduates and nongraduates, but only those who actually attended college classes and who were residents of Southampton when they went to college. I have included students who went to college in New York as well as in New England.

24 The sudden rise in the number of students from Southampton did not result from any dramatic influx of college-age males into the town. Each federal census between 1800

and 1840 listed about 150 males aged fifteen to thirty, an almost constant quarter of Southampton's male population. In the decade when the movement to the colleges reached its peak locally, the number of young men in this age group did not change; the censuses of 1830 and 1840 each listed 154 males aged fifteen to thirty. United States census figures for all of Hampshire, Hampden, and Franklin counties show that Southampton's age pattern followed that of the three-county region almost exactly. The pressure was internal to the town, constant, and quite typical.

25 Edwards, *Address at Southampton*, pp. 27-33; Richardson, *Southampton's Sons*, passim; Samuel L. T. Wright, "Southampton Local History," Typescript, Forbes Library, Northampton, Mass. (1970), p. 95. Wright, who composed his original manuscript between 1881 and 1905, suggested that Gould may have been the major influence behind Southampton's yield of ministers.

26 *Fifty-First Annual Report of the Directors of the American Education Society* (Boston: T. R. Marvin & Son, 1867), p. 12.

27 The following sketch is based on analysis of the family histories and social origins of all fifty Southampton students between 1761 and 1860. The sources for my study were as follows: Chapman, "Chapman Manuscript"; Wright, "Southampton Local History"; Richardson, *Southampton's Sons*; Mrs. Max Lederer, comp., "Vital Records of the Town of Southampton, Massachusetts, 1740-1940," Typescript, Forbes Library, Northampton, Mass. (1942); Atherton W. Parsons, "History of Old Houses," mimeographed (Southampton, Mass.: Southampton Historical Society, 1966); wills and records in Probate Registry, Hall of Records, Northampton, Mass.; and Southampton tax assessment lists for 1810, 1821, 1830, and 1840 in the Treasurer-Collector's Office, Southampton, Mass.

28 It was in the early 1830s that Charles Knowlton, a hill-town doctor in Ashfield, Massachusetts, made his major discoveries in the "anti-conception art" and began to offer instruction to his patients in Ashfield and Hawley (or "Poverty Corners")—just twenty miles north of Southampton. Knowlton related the need for contraception in part to the economic problems he had observed among large families in this area. See Charles Knowlton, *Fruits of Philosophy, or the Private Companion of Adult People*, ed. Norman E. Himes (1832; reprint ed., Mount Vernon, [N.Y.]: Peter Pauper Press, 1937), pp. 10-13, 65-67.

29 Bela Bates Edwards, *Writings of Professor B. B. Edwards, with a Memoir by Edwards A. Park*, 2 vols. (Boston: John P. Jewett & Co., 1853), 1:10-30.

30 Term Bill Ledger A, p. 270, Amherst College Archives, Amherst, Mass.; Montague, *Biographical Record of Amherst*, p. 221.

31 Chapman, "Chapman Manuscript," 1:152; Richardson, *Southampton's Sons*, pp. 145-49; Wright, "Southampton Local History," pp. 130-31; Southampton Tax Assessment, 1821, Treasurer-Collector's Office.

32 Farms of this size would have been about average for inland New England in the early nineteenth century. Bidwell found that the average inland farm ranged between 100 and 200 acres, in a region he considered poor. See Bidwell, "Rural Economy," pp. 321, 371.

33 Edwards, *Writings*, 1:10-30; will of Elisha Edwards, July 12, 1826, Box 53, no. 20, Probate Registry; Chapman, "Chapman Manuscript," 1:89; Richardson, *Southampton's Sons*, pp. 93-106; Southampton Tax Assessment, 1821, Treasurer-Collector's Office.

34 Will of Paul Chapman, September 30, 1852, Box 181, no. 50, Probate Registry; Chapman, "Chapman Manuscript," 1:40-43; Richardson, *Southampton's Sons*, pp. 32-37; Southampton Tax Assessment, 1830, Treasurer-Collector's Office; Edwards, *Address at Southampton*, p. 49. Bidwell determined that the majority of inland farmers with 100 acres might have a total money income of $400 or $500 per year, almost all of which would be expended for necessities; see Bidwell, "Agricultural Revolution," pp. 698-99.

35 Will of Joel Pomeroy, May 2, 1845, Box 116, no. 11, Probate Registry; Chapman, "Chapman Manuscript," 1:210; Richardson, *Southampton's Sons*, pp. 161-64; Southampton Tax Assessment, 1821, Treasurer-Collector's Office.

36 Student Register, 1825-26 to 1835-36, Amherst Archives; "Records of the Hampshire Charitable Society and of the Directors," August 7, 1823, and October 12, 1825, Hampshire Education Society Papers, Forbes Library, Northampton, Mass.; Beneficiary Account Book, beneficiary no. 918, American Education Society Archives, Congregational Library, Boston, Mass.

37 Southampton Tax Assessment, 1821, Treasurer-Collector's Office; will of Joel Pomeroy, May 2, 1845, Box 116, no. 11, Probate Registry. The family of Jairus Burt (Amherst, 1824) actually ranked higher than Pomeroy's, but Burt's father died before he became a beneficiary, making him technically an orphan and placing him in a less advantageous position than Pomeroy.

38 Chapman, "Chapman Manuscript," 1:64, 67; inventory of the estate of Eli Clapp, July 12, 1809, Box 29, no. 18, Probate Registry; Richardson, *Southampton's Sons*, pp. 39-42; "Records of the Hampshire Charitable Society," November 6, 1816, May 15, 1817, December 23, 1817, April

28, 1818, and November 3, 1819, Hampshire Education Society Papers; *Second Annual Report of the Education Society of* *Connecticut* (New Haven: Nathan Whiting, 1818), p. 7.

2 The Experience of Student Poverty

And while I would never beg unless misfortune had thrown me into the most forlorn situation, neither would I reject the kindness of friends when performed with a proper spirit.

John Todd (Yale, 1822)

During his years at college, while he produced no income, a student had traditionally received financial support from the family—an arrangement so common that in the early nineteenth century it still seemed natural. Money for tuition and expenses came from home. Through affection or ambition, or for the sake of tradition, fathers would provide. Yet, there had always been exceptions; the poor, who got little or nothing from their families, had enrolled at Harvard and Yale throughout the colonial period. They were not a demographic novelty peculiar to the nineteenth century, except in their numbers. So when a penniless scholar named John Todd departed for Yale College in the fall of 1818, he confronted what was almost a timeless situation.

For generations, students in Todd's circumstances had been accepting certain forms of charity and patronage as substitutes for family support. They had become wards or protégés of wealthy individuals, the beneficiaries of individual churches, or recipients of college charity funds. And while none of these familiar forms of charity disappeared entirely after 1800, new arrangements—like those made by the education societies—suddenly appeared on a grand scale, altering the experience and even the definition of student poverty. As the directors of the American Education Society defined the terms, students who received the patronage of a church, a relative, or a fortunate friend did not qualify as *poor* or *indigent*.[1] Any student who enjoyed these older forms of support knew a kind of poverty different from that of a self-supporting schoolkeeper or the beneficiary of an education society.

It was in the early nineteenth century that certain changes occurred in the experience of student poverty. A new kind of impoverished scholar appeared, scarcely genteel, and—owing to the necessities of his existence—much closer to the image of the Yankee. A change in experience is an elusive thing to describe; personal detail is needed to evoke the lives and feelings of poor students. One must compare closely their different modes of life, using biographical materials of young men exceptional only because they left literary traces about their youth. The lives of Marshall Henshaw, Mark Hopkins, and John Todd represented three distinctive types of student careers, yet all three young men confronted a social situation common to poor students in the early nineteenth century.

Their lives suggest what the "laggards" were doing during their lost years, when they should have been studying but were not. Their biographies explain why it took some students longer then to reach college and complete their schooling, an explanation always including the impediments of poverty. They reveal changes in the lives and opportunities of young men and—in the cases of Hopkins and Todd—the despairs behind their occasional somber moods. Above all, the biographies disclose existential problems in the lives of Hopkins and Todd especially, problems caused, not by the idiosyncrasies of their personal histories, but by an institutional vacuum peculiar to their time. Traditional arrangements like the scholarship or the town charity fund played no part in their lives. Their stories show how individual students coped with the institutional vacuum, and how that vacuum—together with the new arrangements created to fill it—shaped their lives.

Marshall Henshaw: Protégé

With comfortable clothing and twenty-seven dollars in money, I set out to work my way through college, expecting to teach school in winter to pay my first term's board, and trusting in a kind providence for the future.

Marshall Henshaw (Amherst, 1845)

Eli Henshaw left West Brookfield in Worcester County, Massachusetts, in 1816 to escape the "irksome authority" of his father and to remove himself from a town suffering the same dearth of opportunity that was driving the youth of Southampton into the West. This was five years before the founding of Amherst College, just over the hills from West Brookfield. Henshaw settled in Wayne County, Pennsylvania, where his son Marshall, one of four surviving brothers and five surviving children, was born in 1820. They lived in wilderness fashion, "working hard and faring poorly," as Marshall later recalled. He did attend district school and an academy, but he was himself teaching school by the age of sixteen, and receiving ten dollars a month and "board around." Not until the age of twenty-one did he consider higher education or begin to prepare for it. Then, abruptly, he was dispatched to the college at Amherst, where there were relatives to receive him. Apart from twenty-seven dollars and his clothing, he had nothing; he expected to work his way by keeping school.

None of this proved necessary, for Providence provided. In Henshaw's home town of Bethany, Pennsylvania, lived Major Jason Torrey, an elder in the church, a man, like Silas Sheldon of Southampton, with few family claims and some money to spare. Shortly after arriving in Amherst, Marshall Henshaw received from Major Torrey enough money to pay for his first term's board. Henshaw became Torrey's protégé, depending on the major for the regular financial support that allowed him to finish a full college course—at age twenty-five, but without interruption. It is not known whether he ever expected to repay his patron, except in gratitude and achievement.[2]

At least one piece of correspondence that passed between patron and protégé in these years has survived, and it suggests that a kind of familial relationship developed during Henshaw's period of dependency. He appears to have written to Torrey whenever he needed money, and he accounted for his expenditures.

> At the commencement of the term, I began to board in a club, suposing [*sic*] I should not be able to pay $1.50 per week, which is the usual price in private families. But my cousin Allen, having a debt against a man who keeps a boarding house in the village, & the man being slack in paying his debts, offered to let me board on his account & pay him $1.25 per week, while he allows the man $1.50.

He acknowledged receiving thirty dollars from Torrey: "This money will carry me safe through this term." Henshaw described his interest in religious affairs, assured his patron of his good deportment, and reported on his progress in study. ("I must confess I have some ambition to take a high appointment.") In turn, it appears that when Torrey sent money, he also included fatherly suggestions; Henshaw accepted a kind of paternal supervision along with the patronage. "It gave me great pleasure," he said, "to hear from & receive the advice of one, who had manifested so much friendship for me & is so capable of giving good counsel."[3]

Marshall Henshaw realized this patronage more by chance than by choice; he determined very little by his own will. While his intelligence and success as a teacher in Wayne County no doubt contributed to his visibility back home, he found his favored position chiefly by good luck. Still, many other instances of this kind of chance arrangement between patrons and protégés occurred in the nineteenth century and earlier, both in America and in Europe. It was an old form of patronage.

Occasionally, the student in these circumstances became the legal ward of his patron, and the relationship assumed a greater intimacy. Relations between patrons and wards did not differ in essence from the ordinary ties of family, especially in a time when young servants, orphans, and wards commonly were taken into households and given a status almost indistinguishable from that of the other children. Nor did the relationship differ markedly from other forms of patronage that had appeared at colonial Harvard and Yale, whether the patron was a stranger—as in Henshaw's case—a relative, or a church and its minister. The student merely assumed the role of a son—dependent, grateful, but usually owing nothing more than filial duties.[4]

For example, Mather Byles of the Harvard class of 1725 was treated like the adopted son of his uncle, Cotton Mather. Byles's father, a Boston saddler who moved up the social scale by marrying Mather's sister, died when his son was a year old, leaving only a moderate estate out of which to provide for the boy. The Mathers saw to his educational preparation, and, when he was fourteen and ready for college, his uncle drew upon wealthy friends to finance his course at Harvard, from which he graduated four years later, having received aid from the Hollis and Hulton funds.[5]

Joseph Seccombe, who graduated with the class of 1731, was less fortunate in the circumstances of his birth. His father was "a very obscure innholder" in Boston, and his only connections were through his mother, a member of the Old South Church, from whose charity funds he was educated. In 1726 those funds financed his study under Samuel Wigglesworth; he drew upon them throughout college, supplementing them with additions from the Hollis funds. The reasons for his slightly delayed education—he was born in 1706, did not begin to prepare until he was twenty, and did not graduate until he was twenty-five—are not clear. Perhaps he had to wait his turn upon the church funds; perhaps he simply came to a belated decision, as had Benjamin Prat of the class of 1737. Whatever the explanation for Seccombe's delay, his support once he had started was secure for the whole course.[6]

In cases like Seccombe's, it was common for church and minister to maintain a close relationship with their beneficiary. The number of students who could be enrolled upon the charity funds of a single church was never large, seldom more than one or two; and while the beneficiary selected by the church might be expected to prepare for the ministry, the obligations beyond this—and natural gratitude—were few.[7] The relationship, though more formal than that known by Marshall Henshaw, was nonetheless an intimate one, especially since the young man selected for church patronage usually had grown up in that church and was known to its members. To administer small-scale arrangements like these, it was not necessary to create a large, impersonal system of bureaucratic arrangements like that which appeared in the early nineteenth century.[8]

For poor students like Seccombe, Byles, or Henshaw who experienced these old forms of patronage, the course of education was not essentially different from that followed by students whose parents could provide full support. Though poor and occasionally older, and obviously of a lesser social standing, they shared a common, familial dependence upon the adults who provided their support, and they could know the same security as their more fortunate classmates. By the standards of the nineteenth century, they had scarcely experienced poverty at all. Only a very few of them could have known anything of the delays and disappointments, the uncertainty, the uprootedness, the burden of debt, or the need for virtuosity that became associated with such stereotypes of the Yankee character as Washington Irving's Ichabod Crane and that were essential features of the indigence experienced by several thousand New England students in the first six decades of the nineteenth century.

Mark Hopkins: Laggard

I am, as you will see by the date of this, within two days of being 27 years old, but I am very far from being what I hoped to be at that age. This I impute partly to my own faults, and partly to circumstances beyond my controul.

Mark Hopkins (Williams, 1824)

As Mark Hopkins approached the age of thirty, he became increasingly aware of the length of time it was taking him to get his education. His entrance to college had been delayed three years. There were further delays before he began his abbreviated study of medicine—a study that was not completed until he was twenty-nine and that brought him little success. He was to be well into his thirties before he finally completed his study for the ministry. He tried to be judicious in his assessment of the causes of his slowness and obvious failure: "This I impute partly to my own faults, and partly to circumstances beyond my controul."[9] Occasionally he cited his own lack of energy, his lack of desire to study; with greater frequency he mentioned his low spirits and ill health, which appear to have had more of the character of symptoms than of agents. His failure must have seemed especially painful when he considered that his family had begun to prepare and sacrifice for his education when he was a boy of thirteen.

The delays and disappointments that beset Mark Hopkins, that extended his education into the years of his maturity, are chronicled in the correspondence that passed between him and his family throughout his extended period of education. Often crowded two and three to a single sheet of paper, the letters testify to a scarcity of even the most elementary requirements for nourishing intellectual life. Their contents record each measure taken to prepare him for college and the efforts of his parents in supporting their son as a student. They reveal much about the situation of other bright young men like Mark Hopkins in western Massachusetts between 1815 and 1830, men whose families could not send them to college and whose communities provided none of the familiar forms of patronage enjoyed by Marshall Henshaw, Joseph Seccombe, or Mather Byles. No matter how personal and idiosyncratic his own failures might have seemed to him, Mark Hopkins confronted obstacles that were real and environmental, however dimly he may have perceived them. Still, great as were the difficulties, the Hopkins family correspondence suggests that an inventiveness in overcoming problems characterized both parents and children in this period, thus contributing to the national folk-lore the theme of the aspiring student doggedly pursuing his studies in an effort toward a better life.

Mark Hopkins came from one of those poor New England farm families that provided Yankee schoolteachers for the eighteenth and nineteenth centuries. His parents' farm in Stockbridge, Massachusetts, at the western edge of New England, seems barely to have supported Archibald and Mary Hopkins and their three sons. There, Mark Hopkins was born in 1802, his brother Harry in 1804, and Albert in 1807. Certainly the apples, sheep, and grain grown on the farm could not have sustained three mature sons as farmers, or even provided enough to establish them as farmers in the vicinity, given the competition from the new farms in the West. Nor could it provide enough cash to educate those sons for a profession.

Other obstacles dimmed Mark's prospects for education. During the years in which he ought to have been preparing for college, Stockbridge appears to have supported schools only intermittently.[10] Thus, in order to prepare, it was necessary to cover, in addition to the cost of tuition, the expenses of traveling and of living away from home. The church in Stockbridge appears not to have had a charity fund to help such a scholar; and even if it had, the Hopkinses—who were marginal communicants at best, and whose sons had no ambition toward the ministry—must have been among the least likely candidates for its benevolence. There were no rich uncles among the Hopkins relatives, and they had no wealthy friends. Therefore, the normal channels of support were closed to Mark Hopkins.

He did belong to a family, however, living within a day's ride of Williams College. Moreover, they shared enough of his ambition to make every member willing to sacrifice for one another's advancement. Those sacrifices would mean delays, but, in the end, his family's cooperation would prove invaluable.

The motives that prompted the Hopkinses to plan and struggle for the education of Mark and Albert are simple enough to understand, given the alternatives. It was impossible for all three sons to farm the Hopkins homestead; if they had continued in their father's pursuit, at least two boys would have found it necessary to join the westward migration, a move already undertaken by some of their relatives—Archibald's brother Sewall, for one. The terrors of the western journey had been vividly described to the Hopkinses in letters from these relatives. Besides, Archibald and Mary Hopkins wanted to keep their family together near home, probably in part because their sons were their major source of security for old age.[11] The Hopkinses were an affectionate family. When her sons were away, Mary wrote them of her dreams that they had returned and were together again. Still, they could not stay near home as farmers; Archibald and Mary assumed from the start that their sons would leave the farm and that, within the lifetime of one generation, the Hopkinses of Stockbridge would cease to be a farming family.

To abandon farming and to refuse to join the westward movement meant that other work must be found. It also meant that the Hopkins sons would undoubtedly require a good deal of education and professional training, facts which began to concern the parents when the boys were still quite young.

Their early letters are filled with accounts of books read by firelight, volumes of classics finished, recitations passed, languages self-taught, discussions after the day's work. The Hopkinses seem always to have had an intellectual energy that even their daily chores could not consume.

Mark Hopkins was fortunate also in having an uncle, Sewall Hopkins, who, while poor, was willing to shelter him while he prepared for college, in exchange for work on Sewall's farm in Clinton, New York. Thus the first step in Mark's preparation was a conventional one; it is recorded in the family correspondence of 1815, when Mark, at the age of thirteen, went west to live with his uncle. Clinton, to which town Sewall had moved by 1789, was a farming community about 100 miles west of Stockbridge.[12] In 1812 the town became the site of Hamilton College, making it thus doubly attractive to the Stockbridge Hopkinses. The text of the correspondence suggests that the notion of sending Mark to Clinton actually may have originated with Sewall Hopkins and that he simply proposed in the fall of 1814 that Archibald send him an able-bodied son.

> The case with me is this: I have sometimes a man 6 or 8 months and sometimes I am destitute—I have no boy at present—If you think of giving Mark a liberal education, he would be young enough to enter college at the commencement of his 17th year, if I mistake not he must be about 13 now. . . . If Mark should come and live with me I think I could board him and fit him to enter college at 17 for the assistance he might render me, and not interfere with his studies provided you clothe him.[13]

Unlike Sewall, who had no sons old enough to work his farm, Archibald Hopkins had too many. The Stockbridge farm seems to have functioned with the labor of two men, plus the part-time, seasonal service of a hired man. Thus, Archibald had two extra sons much of the year. If Mark were to be educated, his services could be spared while he was sent away to Clinton.[14]

The letters that passed between Stockbridge and Clinton in 1815 and 1816 give a clear picture of what it took to prepare a poor boy for college, financially and scholastically. They make the farming-out arrangement seem all the more necessary and suggest why delays might be expected by a student in Mark Hopkins's circumstances.

Clinton had a grammar school that prepared scholars to enter the college. According to Sewall's letter of March 26, 1815, these scholars boarded with various families in the town. Charges at the grammar school, which Mark described as having "not a very good school house," were five dollars tuition per year.[15] College students customarily lived in a college building and ate meals either at a dining hall, when there was one, or with families in town. According to Sewall, they paid two dollars and twenty-five cents a week for meals, washing, wood, and candles. He added lodging to this list, probably by mistake: the college charged them ten dollars per quarter for tuition and room.[16]

Sewall agreed to board Mark at three or four shillings a week less than the rate at the Steward's House, where most Hamilton students dined in 1815.

In return, Mark worked on the farm. Since one term of thirteen weeks was vacation each year—a fairly new arrangement in the collegiate calendar, provided to assist such students as Mark Hopkins—Sewall predicted that Mark could earn enough for wood, candles, and books in that period. If Archibald could provide Mark with $120 a year plus his clothes and traveling expenses, Sewall estimated, "it would I believe cover every expense you would be at if the times are as they are at present."[17] Archibald was not at all certain he could raise $120 in cash for even a single year, but he bowed to his son's desires and wrote that he was permitting him to proceed with his preparations.

> You wish to know what course to take in your future studies and whether you are eventually to go to Collidge. We have been consulting on that subject and concluded that you had better begin to study Latin and such other studies as your instructor shall think proper for a beginner. . . . Whether I shall be able to carry you through will depend on my circumstances. It will be soon enough for you to enter coledge when you are 17 years ould, that is a long time yet and if you improve what time you have you may well be fitted to enter by that time. We have concluded to have you stay one year or more longer before you come home, though that will be a long while.[18]

Delays were built into the work-study arrangements devised by Sewall and Archibald. "I have begun to study Latin but it will take me a long time to get fitted for college," Mark wrote, "for if I stay here I shall probably have to stay away from school one third of the time—or more."[19] His daily schedule often conflicted with a scholar's needs, no matter how he might try to improve his time. Morning chores lasted till ten o'clock. "I then begin to study in the midst of a very great confusion and study till noon." Afternoon chores preceded two more hours of study between two and four. Only his evenings were really good for study, he wrote his father, "so that you may easily perceive that I make but poor proficiency." Nevertheless, between planting, hoeing, and haying for his uncle, he tried to prepare himself for college.[20]

Probably the Hopkinses had decided after a few months that these arrangements were not satisfactory and that, indeed, they would bring Mark home after a year or so of preparation at Clinton, instead of leaving him with his uncle Sewall to study at Hamilton College.[21] As the end of the first year approached, it became evident that while Sewall was anxious to keep Mark, his parents wanted him to return, and that Mark was divided in his sentiments, since he clearly saw that his best chance for beginning a collegiate education at the age of seventeen lay in the arrangements at Clinton.

In April 1816, Mark and his uncle shared a sheet of paper to write Mark's parents. Mark outlined his most recent expenses, and Sewall rehearsed all the arguments in favor of keeping Mark in Clinton, where he might enter college at seventeen, be well prepared "without being constantly at school," and earn his way by working on the farm. "As the expense of his going home & return cannot be less than 20$ I advise him not to go at present but he will do as you say & he wishes for you to write immediately."[22]

Sometime in April 1816, Archibald Hopkins decided that he could not send Mark to college after all and called him home. Sewall pictured Mark as receiving the intelligence with gloom, and he made one final appeal. It was his belief, he said, that a liberal education would be "the best portion" that Archibald could give his son. It would permit him to go through life with intellectual "enjoyment," make him more useful to mankind, and "fit him to be useful in any station in life." Then he offered some practical advice.

If you should find yourself likely to be straightened for money after he enters College, had you not better part with some of your landed property & charge Mark with the expense of his education as so much towards his portion; it will be better for him to make his way in the world than so much cash given him without it.[23]

Mark found the idea of an education in return for a portion of his inheritance entirely satisfactory. To his uncle's letter he appended the brief message: "I had much rather have a liberal Education and nothing else than to have considerable more money than to carry me through—but if you want my help I know that I owe a great debt and am willing to pay what I can—you know better than I concerning these things."[24] Views similar to these had prompted Archibald and Mary to send Mark to Clinton in the first place, but circumstances prevented completion of the plan, and Mark returned to Stockbridge sometime in 1816. For this reason, he did not begin his college education at age seventeen.

Four years after his return to Stockbridge, when he was eighteen and had little prospect of starting college, Mark Hopkins took a job as a schoolteacher in a family school in Virginia, the kind of work universally found by students who had to finance their own educations in the early nineteenth century. Both of Mark's brothers taught school at different times, never with any pleasure. Harry Hopkins taught under an arrangement by which he was expected to board at every home in the district for four or five days at a time. He and Mark both complained of interruptions and of the difficulty of studying while teaching, which only compounded the delay. "I do not wish you the happiness ever to teach school," Mark once wrote to his brother.[25]

For teaching between eleven and twenty-two scholars at different times, Mark hoped to earn $400, clear of expenses, in about one year, which was about average for a full-time teacher in his position. In other words, for one year's work he could buy two years at college, if he scrimped. If he stayed another half year, his employers promised him $640 before expenses. The effect of an additional delay upon his admission to Williams College worried him most. "If it were certain that I could enter with the Sophomores at the end of winter vacation it would probably be best for me to remain," he wrote his mother, "but my age is now such that should I not be able to enter with them I shall hardly finish my education at all."[26] Reluctantly, he decided that he would need more money; therefore, he determined to teach the additional months, returning to western Massachusetts sometime in December 1821. Evidently, he entered Williams College in January 1822. His first letter from Williamstown was dated February 28, just twenty-four days after his twentieth birthday.

Although he was beginning his college education three years later than he had hoped, the college eased his situation somewhat by permitting him to enter in the middle of his sophomore year. By preparation in the classics, a few students did gain admission to New England colleges with advanced standing, after performing well in entrance examinations. Thus a man who could not enter at the customary age of seventeen could gain time—if he could find a tutor, could attend an academy, or could teach himself.[27] If he were quite mature, his age might work in his favor in gaining advanced standing. Mark's younger brother, Albert, took similar advantage of the opportunity to gain advanced standing in the spring of 1824, when he entered Williams as a sophomore at the age of sixteen.[28] Albert had the benefit of other factors as well. His family had been as solicitous about his preparation as they had been about Mark's. Mark was nearly finished at Williams when Albert began, and he had financed much of his own education, not drawing heavily upon his parents. The second Hopkins son, Harry, showed no scholarly inclination and seemed uninterested in pursuing his fortune through higher education, so the family was spared this expense. Thus Albert Hopkins derived advantages from his position as the youngest son and began his studies at Williams at a tender age. This was just what Mark had been hoping for; since 1821, he had been worrying about his brothers.

> I trust Albert will not have so great a load of poverty on his back that he shall be obliged to hover as long and as vexatiously about the doors of a college before he shall be able to enter as I have done. . . .[29]

Furthermore, by the time Albert was ready to begin at Williams, the Hopkinses had adopted certain financial measures that enabled the family to function as a mutual aid society, strengthening the bonds of affection with new ties of economic interdependence. Other families in New England at this time were engaging in similar practices. For the Hopkinses, this scheme was foreshadowed when Mark was sent to Sewall's farm in Clinton. To have a relative living in another part of the country, where regional agricultural and educational conditions might be better, was an advantage that could be pressed—even by the poor—whenever family ties had not broken completely.

The Hopkins family really began its mutual aid enterprises shortly after Mark entered Williams, with brother helping brother and parents and sons assisting one another at different times. Mark received some assistance from the family, though he relied chiefly on his own earnings. After his graduation, Mark accepted a tutorship at Williams; with the amount he earned, perhaps $500, he could send money home and to his brother Harry when Harry was studying art in New York. When Albert began studies at Williams, Mark probably helped finance him and secure him a tutorship after graduation. When Mark then went to New York to study medicine after two years as a tutor, the whole family assisted him. Each brother shared his parents' desire to see everyone "set up" in a profession, and each took his turn at preparing and supporting another. With Mark giving up his portion of the family estate in return for help with his education, and with all three sons contributing to their mutual advancement, the Hopkinses provided for themselves. This arrangement, differing from the total support of a student that was customary in more affluent families, merely contributed to the delays in Mark's career.

Significantly, Mark Hopkins's advanced age did not make him unique among his classmates, nor, indeed, among New England college students in general. In Hopkins's class of 1824, more than half the members were over twenty-four. Mark, at twenty-two and a half, was among the youngest of its fifteen members. It is probable that anyone Mark's age or older had shared at least some of his difficulties in getting into college and had devised similar means to conquer those difficulties. Nine of his classmates were his age or older. Henry Davis, the only graduate under twenty, was the son of President Davis of Hamilton College and a close friend of Edward Dorr Griffin, the Williams president. Davis, John Staniford Robinson, and Seth Moar were probably the only members of this class who had no difficulty in completing their education at Williams. Two of the oldest members, Eli Adams and Alvah Lilly (both twenty-seven), had required the assistance of the American Education Society; their relatively advanced age was typical for A.E.S. beneficiaries, whose correspondence with the society was filled with tales of late starts and delays.[30]

The broad discrepancies between ages in the class of 1824 were also evident in Albert Hopkins's class of 1826, and were even more extreme when one considers the ages of all the college's students at any given time. At various times in the 1820s, the student body at Williams included boys of fifteen as well as married men in their thirties. (One member of Albert Hopkins's class was married and had a family.)[31] By the early nineteenth century, especially at the provincial colleges of New England, students of Mark Hopkins's age were quite common, their life histories displaying similar interruptions and delays. Their poverty was producing a new kind of student career.

John Todd: Ichabod

My circumstances make me turn my hand to almost any thing; but I care not, as it teaches me to do business, to see society, to be placed in different situations, to see men and manners in all their varieties.

John Todd (Yale, 1822)

John Todd was born on October 9, 1800. When he was about six, his father died, leaving an insane widow and seven orphans, who were scattered wherever places could be found for them. The father, an ill-educated, itinerant physician who had moved the family from town to town in Connecticut and Vermont in search of business, left his family no estate, no church connection, and no permanent home. He did have many friends and relatives, among whom his son John passed a vagabond youth. Between the ages of six and twelve, he spent most of his time with his aunt and uncle Hamilton at North Killing-worth, Connecticut, in hill country. In the winter of 1810, his aunt broke up her household while his uncle, a sailor, was being held prisoner by the Spanish; John was sent to live in New Haven with an older cousin, Jeremiah Evarts. Evarts was then struggling to establish a law practice in New Haven; to make ends meet, he took in boarders from the college. John waited on table, ran errands, and received some schooling in exchange. In the spring, he returned to the Hamiltons.[32]

When he was twelve, John Todd moved in with another uncle, his father's brother, Dr. Jonathan Todd, at East Guilford, "that I might enjoy better means of schooling, my opportunities having as yet been small." In 1815 he begged Evarts to accept him once more as a member of the latter's family, Evarts having moved to Charlestown, Massachusetts, where the opportunities for schooling were even greater. Evarts consented, and in November Todd walked to Boston. In the Evarts household, Todd performed the duties of a servant, sawing wood, drawing water, running errands, and eventually doing routine office work for Evarts.[33]

In April 1817, Todd was converted during a religious revival which took place in Charlestown, and he determined to go to college and prepare for the ministry. His relatives did little to assist him. Evarts wrote him a letter of introduction to the American Education Society, then sent him off to walk to New Haven in the fall of 1818 without further assistance. His uncle Jonathan Todd refused to sign his college bond. John Todd's brother, also named Jonathan Todd but who was as impoverished as young John, signed the bond and Yale, unaware of the apparent fraud, accepted it.[34] Although John's examination was poor, President Day and Professor Kingsley agreed to admit him to the freshman class.

At this point, the consequences of Todd's uprooted youth among poor and reluctant relatives became quite evident. To all those institutions of charity and support that, until the early nineteenth century, had worked at the local level through towns, churches, and schools, John Todd was totally invisible. He had no minister, no teacher, no friend, and no relative who had known him a lifetime and could step forward to assist him. He had spent his life among strangers. His major resources were ambition, wit, and ingenuity—displayed so portentously in his entrance to Yale. The only economic security he enjoyed was the small support he received from the American Education Society, which provided a novel kind of patronage for students whose lives had denied them connections to the old institutions of local or familial support.[35]

Instead of going directly to Yale, Todd might have delayed his education by teaching, as Mark Hopkins had done and as friends advised him to do. However, the minimal aid held forth by the American Education Society may have encouraged him to begin immediately; he might have received as much as fifteen dollars a quarter in 1818 from the A.E.S., a sum the society estimated would pay about half his necessary expenses. (Hopkins had not been eligible for this aid, since he had no desire to study for the ministry when he went to Williams.) Todd was able to start to college almost on schedule, much earlier than Mark; in the process of hurrying through Yale, however, he acquired a comparable kind of maturity and experience.

Apart from the small appropriations he received from the education society, Todd was forced to support himself. Indeed, the A.E.S. encouraged its beneficiaries to rely heavily upon themselves by granting sums that actually provided less than half the necessary support in most cases. The American Education Society encouraged beneficiaries to teach school, work with their hands, or seek the aid of friends. During Todd's years as a beneficiary, the society had not yet devised the schedules upon which later beneficiaries were to submit precise accounts of their incomes and expenditures. The role of the A.E.S. in a beneficiary's life cannot have been very different during 1818-22 from what it was in 1841, however; a few schedules submitted in 1841 by students at Yale have survived and permit at least a general assessment of A.E.S. assistance. By 1841 the quarterly appropriation had risen to $20.00; in a few cases, a double appropriation was granted, but most beneficiaries received the standard allotment. This amount did not cover the total expenses of any Yale student reporting. The quarterly expenses at Yale for nine weeks of study ranged from a low figure of $36.09 reported by H. C. Atwater of the class of 1842, to a high of nearly $120.00. Most expenses ranged between $40.00 and $70.00, and most Yale beneficiaries were in debt to sources other than the A.E.S.[36]

These circumstances encouraged Todd and his fellow beneficiaries to lead vagabond lives, even as students; Todd bragged that he turned his hand "to almost anything." He engaged in a commerce with society that permitted him "to see men and manners in all their varieties." He was away from the college for long periods—with the approval and understanding of President Day—and nearly always had concerns that carried him beyond its walls into the life of New Haven and the surrounding country. Beneficiaries like Todd were constantly on the move. They were absent when agents of the A.E.S. tried to visit them or when it was time for them to submit a quarterly application for aid. "It is wrong that our young men should run about in this manner," an A.E.S. secretary once complained, "but it is difficult to prevent it."[37] A large part of the correspondence between the A.E.S. and its beneficiaries was devoted to the simple problem of making special appropriations to students who had been absent and unable to fill out a schedule at the proper time. It was a routine problem.[38]

During his first winter at Yale, Todd taught school at Hotchkisstown, about two and a half miles from college, walking between school and college while keeping up with his Yale classmates at the same time. There followed a succession of schools and wild boys—in New Haven, Orange, and Fairfield. During his first year, he claimed that he made $160 from his part-time teaching. His students remembered him as a very grave man at eighteen; he was always too busy for college frolics.[39]

His spare time was given to serious concerns. In the summer of 1820, during a revival in New Haven, Todd joined in the work. "He was much engaged in labors to save souls," recalled one of his classmates, "not only among the college students, but everywhere as he had opportunity." In fact, the classmate recalled, "Until the last year he was not as well known by his classmates as others, though he had more acquaintance with the ladies of New Haven than almost any one else." From these ladies, whom Todd undoubtedly met in the course of his religious activities, he received sympathy and occasional benevolence. While teaching in Hotchkisstown, he founded a Sunday school, which he maintained until illness compelled him to cease leading it; it had earned him the sympathy of the Hotchkisstown ladies, however. "As I was poor, the ladies of the neighborhood kindly made me up a small purse to bear my expenses." They gave him $8.90 in money, a pair of boots, two cravats, and some shirts they had fashioned with their own hands. They gave him food, and when he was sick they sent medicines for his cough.[40] For Todd, poverty meant a life of marginal subsistence.

During brief vacations, the problem of finding food and shelter sometimes became especially acute, since there was not enough time for Todd to find work. At these times, and when he was ill—or perhaps just out of money and without means to earn any—he asked to visit his long-lost sisters and sought introduction to the homes of people who had known his father. In 1820 he initiated a correspondence with the Reverend Chauncey Lee of Colebrook, Connecticut, once a friend of his father. He described his illness (a pain in the chest), his poverty, and spoke of his determination to commence a walking tour for his health. "It is my wish to become acquainted with men and manners," he wrote, "and if there are any in Arlington who were acquainted with my father, perhaps they would not be unwilling to see his son." Could Reverend Lee provide him with letters of introduction to any such men? Lee rose to the occasion and invited Todd to Colebrook, as if "to a father's and mother's house." Todd abandoned his plan for the journey to Arlington in favor of Lee's offer.[41]

Todd's quest for this feeble sort of patronage took him as far away as upstate New York and South Carolina, to the latter while college was in session. Similar expeditions contributed to the absenteeism of other beneficiaries, who always described their forays as journeys in search of the aid of "friends."[42] Friends would provide food and shelter; friends would provide travel money; friends would give money and become temporary patrons.[43] In Todd's case, these missions marked his reduction to a medieval style of student living; they were a form of begging.

Todd also borrowed money, either from friends or by signing notes to Yale College for his tuition. In 1822 he owed perhaps $130 for his debts at Yale, a small sum compared to the debts subscribed by many beneficiaries of the American Education Society. Borrowing had become a universal recourse for college students in the early nineteenth century, and many graduates went out into the world burdened with debts they could never repay. Those who did repay had the satisfaction of knowing that they had paid for their education through their own efforts, however long deferred the payment might have been.[44]

By begging and borrowing a bit more from friends, and by earning occasional small sums for preaching and from his part-time work in the library and for a small newspaper, Todd financed three full years at Andover Theological Seminary after leaving Yale.[45] It was largely his own achievement, as he well knew.

> I rose above all; I went to college, half-fitted; I was sick much of the time, owing to too severe application and anxiety; I pressed on, rose above all, and now stand where I can see my way clear.

It was a good thing for John Todd that he never hesitated to help himself or to ask for aid. In his situation, one could not always be delicate. While he would never have begged unless destitute, neither would he have rejected "the kindness of friends."[46] Had he waited for the church to call him, or for a patron to appear, opportunity might well have passed him by. His material needs as a student demanded that he shift for himself, adopt an aggressive demeanor, and enter society as an adult, leaving to others the sheltered life of a college boy. Genteel poverty in the manner of the eighteenth century was very unlike his own experience, for John Todd lived outside the old institutional setting, beyond all traditional means of charitable support. For his time, his life as a student was necessarily a novel one.

Notes

1 The American Education Society maintained a fairly close watch over the income of its beneficiaries, in part to eliminate anyone who received sizable amounts from sources of this kind. For examples, see Hiram Doane to Elias Cornelius, December 25, 1829, and John A. Vinton to Cornelius, January 25, 1830, Beneficiary Letters, American Education Society Archives, Congregational Library, Boston, Mass.

2 George H. Tilton, *A Memorial of Marshall Henshaw* (Cambridge, Mass.: The University Press, 1901), pp. 1-8.

3 Henshaw to Torrey, February 10, 1844, Henshaw folder, Amherst College Archives, Amherst, Mass.; Tilton, *Henshaw*, pp. 8-15.

4 For another example of the patron-ward relationship, see Benjamin Palmer, *The Life and Letters of James Henley Thornwell* (Richmond, Va.: Whittet & Shepperson, 1875), pp. 18-71.

5 Clifford K. Shipton, *Sibley's Harvard Graduates*, vol. 7 (Boston: Massachusetts Historical Society, 1945), pp. 464-66; compare also the case of Jonathan Sewall (Harvard, 1748), in ibid., vol. 12 (Boston: Massachusetts Historical Society, 1962), pp. 306-25.

6 Ibid., vol. 9 (Boston: Massachusetts Historical Society, 1956), pp. 87-88, and vol. 10 (Boston: Massachusetts Historical Society, 1958), pp. 226-28.

7 Occasionally, the members of a church might expect their beneficiary to remain orthodox in doctrine, as in the case of a Connecticut church that refused to support young men after one of its beneficiaries became an "infidel." Erastus Dickinson to Samuel Riddel, October 2, 1848, Beneficiary Letters, A.E.S. Archives.

8 Nor were large-scale arrangements necessary when patronage was administered by a college, particularly in the pre-Revolutionary period. For a discussion of the college as a patron, see Chapter 3 of this text.

9 Mark Hopkins, *Early Letters of Mark Hopkins, and Others from His Brothers and Their Mother: A Picture of Life in New England from 1770 to 1857*, ed. S. S. H. (New York: John Day Company, 1929), p. 187.

10 Harry wrote Mark on November 9, 1815, that he had attended school only a few days in the previous year and a half. See ibid., p. 30.

11 Ibid., pp. 35-43.

12 Ibid., p. 2.

13 Ibid., p. 15.

14 In this respect, Mark Hopkins's situation was almost like that of a rural youth in preindustrial England. Peter Laslett has traced the life cycle of a poor young inhabitant of an English village in *The World we have lost* (New York: Charles Scribner's Sons, 1965), pp. 14-16. English agricul-

ture, Laslett suggests, required a similar pool of labor on a seasonal basis, leaving a surplus for part of the year. Extra sons left home between the ages of ten and twelve, usually to become servants to others in the area.

15 Hopkins, *Early Letters*, pp. 15, 17.

16 Ibid., p. 15.

17 Ibid., pp. 33-34.

18 Ibid., pp. 27-28.

19 Ibid., p. 28.

20 Ibid., pp. 34-35. On August 29, 1815, he reported that he had spent one week planting, one week hoeing, and seven weeks haying and that he had not been in school for some time; ibid., p. 23.

21 See Archibald Hopkins to Mark Hopkins, September 11, 1815, ibid., pp. 27-28.

22 Ibid., pp. 31-32.

23 Ibid., pp. 33-34.

24 Ibid., p. 34.

25 Ibid., pp. 98, 61-62, 85.

26 Ibid., p. 75.

27 Mark Hopkins's preparation included all three methods. He attended the academies at Clinton and Lenox, taught himself in Virginia, and was tutored for a time by an uncle, Jared Curtis (Williams, 1800). See Calvin Durfee, *Williams Biographical Annals* (Boston: Lee and Shepard, 1871), pp. 31, 228.

28 Ibid., p. 147.

29 Hopkins, *Early Letters*, p. 87.

30 Durfee, *Williams Annals*, pp. 414-19, 128-30; see also Beneficiary Account Book, A.E.S. Archives, which contains the names of beneficiaries, numbered 1 through 2,700. (Eli Adams was no. 235, Alvah Lilly, no. 313.) The A.E.S. received numerous letters like that from John A. Vinton, a student at Andover Theological Seminary when he wrote the secretary in 1830: "Until the age of 21 years, I lived with my father. . . . Not the least prospect, however, appeared of ever obtaining an education: as my father never encouraged my desire for it, but often told me that his circumstances would not allow him to render me any assistance in obtaining it." Vinton to Elias Cornelius, January 25, 1830, Beneficiary Letters, A.E.S. Archives.

31 Durfee, *Williams Annals*, p. 426; Hopkins, *Early Letters*, p. 117.

32 John E. Todd, ed., *John Todd: The Story of His Life, Told Mainly by Himself* (New York: Harper & Brothers, 1876), pp. 19-45.

33 Ibid., pp. 48, 53-57.

34 Ibid., pp. 63-66.

35 It is important to realize that a student did not have to be uprooted geographically to be removed from these institutions in the early nineteenth century. Such deprivation could be experienced even in some New England towns where churches had grown feeble.

36 Secretary's return, Connecticut Branch of the American Education Society, July 1841, Beneficiary Letters, A.E.S. Archives. Some expenses lower than Atwater's were reported, but they were for fewer weeks of study. Most Yale students in this report had studied for nine weeks, though the range was from one to thirteen. Only a small amount was reported for teaching and labor in this return; little income of this nature could be expected for the quarter ending in July, since most work was found in winter, for which no schedules survive.

37 William Cogswell to Benjamin Labaree, November 4, 1837, Letter Book 2, A.E.S. Archives.

38 See Waters Warren to Elias Cornelius, November 17, 1827; Alvah Steele to Cornelius, December 10, 1827; John Taylor Jones to Cornelius, January 2, 1828; William Allen to Cornelius, February 19, 1830; John Parker to Cornelius, February 28, 1830; Oliver W. Goodwin to the directors, December 1, 1830; Henry H. Smith to B. B. Edwards, October 3, 1831; George Clark to William Cogswell, July 7, 1840; James A. Brainerd to Cogswell, September 9, 1840; and Jared R. Swift to Cogswell, August 24, 1840; all in Beneficiary Letters, A.E.S. Archives.

39 Todd, *John Todd*, pp. 68-69, 93.

40 Ibid., pp. 72, 74, 79, 93.

41 Ibid., pp. 75-77.

42 For example, see Aaron N. Colton to Elias Cornelius, March 18, 1831, Beneficiary Letters, A.E.S. Archives. Colton, a Yale student, was writing from northern Vermont after an excursion to Philadelphia and Washington in search of health, teaching jobs, and friends who would support him.

43 The item covering this source of funds on the A.E.S. schedule was titled, "Received from other public funds & from friends." Though the sums under this heading were quite large in the Yale schedules for July 1841, it is impossible to tell what portion came from public funds and what portion from friends. It is obvious that the applicants did not expect to repay a large percentage of the money they received under this heading, since they did not include much of it in their total debts. J. Augustine Benton, for example, had received seventy dollars from "other public funds & from friends," but he listed only twenty-five dollars as his present debt, exclusive of that owed to the A.E.S. See secretary's return, Connecticut Branch, July 1841, Beneficiary Letters, A.E.S. Archives.

44 Todd, *John Todd*, p. 94.

45 Ibid., pp. 94, 105-07, 117, 119-20.

46 Ibid., pp. 79, 118.

PART II

Charity as a Lever of Change

New England grew poorer between 1760 and 1860 in its traditional resources for supporting impoverished scholars. Wells of charity that had been working for a century and more ran dry, in part because of a drought in American philanthropy, in part because of the increasing demand on more wells. Old sources of aid—intimate, familial arrangements for charity made in separate little communities, churches, and colleges—could not provide sufficient support for indigent scholars in the early nineteenth century. A major change occurred after 1800 in the material conditions of higher education for the poor.

The poor appeared in colleges in larger numbers, despite a decline in scholarships and in the meager charity funds maintained by the churches. These sources, which once determined the number of charity students, diminished in importance. Yet growth in the number of poor students did take place, through personal sacrifice and through great institutional change.

The presence of these young men was revealed in the changes they prompted in the administration and distribution of educational charity in New England. As individual communities lost their role in supporting scholars, patronage of the poor ceased to be an act of individual charity, rendered in personal, paternal fashion. Patronage became a matter of organized regional and national benevolence, controlled by bureaucratic institutions. As college funds were overwhelmed, the locus of power began to shift in higher education. The colleges found themselves weaker, less able to control the composition or behavior of the student population.

Sources outside the communities and colleges sustained the influx by the poor. New charitable institutions appeared to aid them on a scale that changed student life, extending to indigent students an unprecedented degree of self-determination and choice in matters pertaining to education and vocation. At the same time, the new arrangements encouraged still greater numbers of poor young men to enter the student population.

45

3   Ancient Patrons:
Dry Wells

It is not great matters that we aim at, but a competent & necessary sub-sistence for learning according to our day of small things in a wilder-nes.

Jonathan Mitchell, ca. 1663

By an irony of nineteenth-century social history, it was precisely when the poor began to seek admission to New England's colleges that the charitable resources of these institutions were most scarce. Expansion of the student popu-lation and the influx of the poor did not result from a sudden rise in the number of places endowed for the poor. On the contrary, scholarships had disappeared from even the memory of most men.

Thus, while the three histories of Harvard written between 1833 and 1848 speak at length of the gifts that had been given to establish scholarships at Harvard, it is likely that only men who had examined the historical records could have been aware of these funds; for by 1833—with rare exception—the scholarship as a means of "competent & necessary subsistence for learning" was a thing of the past (and future), even at Harvard.[1] So insignificant were the exceptions to this rule, and so impressive were the scholarships founded after midcentury, that the earlier ones were forgotten: "Scholarships have only existed at Harvard since 1852," President Eliot declared with authority in his report for 1875-76.[2] While the Harvard historians knew better, it is evident from their discussions that, until 1852, the scholarship was of historic, not contemporary, significance. In the early nineteenth century, no more than a handful of poor students in American colleges could have received a *scholar-ship*, as the word once had been understood.[3] Rather, any assistance that stu-

46

dents received from the college probably came from charity or from beneficiary funds, whose aid differed from the scholarship in ways that may have been difficult for anyone but a student to detect. Between 1815 and 1850, the colleges did devise loan programs and economical arrangements for food and shelter to assist the poor. After 1850 they began to reinvent the scholarship; for the early nineteenth century, however, this ancient source of support had ceased to function, a state of affairs which was to have significant consequences.

The term *scholarship* has at times been rather imprecise, subject to abuses and stretches of meaning. At one time or another, almost any kind of assistance or charity received by a student has been referred to as a scholarship.[4] From the text of at least one appeal for scholarships at Harvard, however, and from wills and other documents that actually conveyed gifts to Harvard and Yale in the seventeenth and early eighteenth centuries, it is apparent that founders of the original American scholarships used the word with some precision. By 1800, however, it was difficult to find a subsidy matching their definition.

Naturally, their understanding derived almost entirely from British usage; most of the early endowments for scholarships in America came from England (for example, the Hollis and Hopkins foundations at Harvard and the Berkeley at Yale. (The term *exhibition* was employed interchangeably with *scholarship* both in England and America.) In the case of Jonathan Mitchell's appeal for scholarship funds at Harvard, "A Modell For the Maintaining of Students & Fellows of Choise Abilities at the Colledge in Cambridge" (ca. 1663), the English influence could not have been more pronounced. Mitchell copied verbatim whole sections from a similar appeal published in 1658 by Matthew Poole on behalf of Cambridge University. In Mitchell's model, one finds intact the classic definition of a proper scholarship: an annual stipend from an endowed fund, sufficient to maintain a poor scholar at his studies full time. That stipend might not provide complete support; it might only supplement other assistance provided by the college or the family. In any case, Mitchell prohibited his scholars from being "absent from ye Colledge above a month in a yeare unlesse extraordinarily visited by sickness." His scholarship was an appointment of honor, a recognition for boys of choice abilities.[5]

Mitchell envisioned an intimate, local charity. Scholars were to be chosen carefully from within the college or from the schools in surrounding towns, and the funds would be administered locally by the college and trustees from the towns. Scholars would be supervised, so that "no Idle Drones or unworthy & unprofitable persons be hereby maintained." Once the scholarship had been awarded, it might support the scholar through his second degree, providing secure support for a thorough education ("the whole Charge whereof but few parents among us are able or willing to beare of themselves"). While it might rest upon acts of local charity, its financial status did not differ in this respect from an endowed professorship. Once established, its funds, too, became a part of the endowments whose income the college paid to scholars and teachers.

Mitchell knew it would be difficult to establish a proper scholarship in America in 1663, so he "reduced and accommodated" Poole's plan, making it accord with his "day of small things in a wildernes." He expected no large gifts from wealthy benefactors, nor did he fully expect to raise a permanent endowment for his scholarships, for Harvard was already familiar with the peculiar problems of investment and endowment in the wilderness. Prudently, he relied on a subscription drive as a method of financing more appropriate to the economic conditions of the colony.[6]

Exhibitions similar to Mitchell's had been established in large numbers at the English universities by the time Mitchell wrote. By 1660, according to one estimate, 487 scholars were being supported in whole or in part at Oxford and Cambridge, where enrollments were higher than at Harvard. London alone created endowments for 181 scholarships and about 62 fellowships at Oxford and Cambridge.[7]

By 1735 Harvard and Yale, too, had received gifts and bequests to establish scholarships; although these donations were on the order of the model proposed by Mitchell they were not actually prompted by Mitchell himself. In 1712 Harvard received the bequest that Edward Hopkins had willed to the college in 1657; it created four scholarships for graduate students in divinity, permitting them to continue their studies in residence beyond their first degrees.[8]

The donation that Harvard received in 1720 from Thomas Hollis, a London merchant and a Baptist, provided the college with its major fund for undergraduate exhibitions. Hollis specified that stipends of ten pounds should be used for "the maintenance and education of pious young men for the ministry, who are poor in this world." By 1722 Hollis funds were providing those ten pounds a year to each of ten students, seven of them undergraduates. In those days, ten pounds provided a sufficient maintenance, when added to smaller sums a student might have received from his family or the college. Hollis's donation nearly doubled the number of exhibitions that Harvard could offer. In 1722 the college awarded only fourteen other exhibitions, ranging from four to twelve pounds each; and eight of these, having no endowment, had to be paid from general college revenues, making them vulnerable to cancellation.[9]

Bishop Berkeley's scholarship at Yale was almost identical to the Hopkins scholarships at Harvard. In 1733 Berkeley specified that the income from his land in Rhode Island should be paid annually "to three students of the said college, towards their maintenance and subsistence during the time between their first and second degree," with the college to choose the scholars and administer the land. Scholars were obliged to reside in the college three quarters of every year in which they enjoyed the scholarship.[10]

In the case of the Hopkins and Berkeley scholarships—both actually were fellowships—the major intention was, not to aid indigent students, but to promote graduate study, which had virtually disappeared in the colonies. It proved difficult to find students willing to take this money even for a year of graduate work. Harvard had trouble finding "suitable persons to fill up ye number" of Hopkins scholarships in 1735, 1741, 1743, 1747, 1748, and 1749.[11] Yale made annual appointments on Berkeley's funds until 1782, when Ezra Stiles recorded the first instance in which no candidate could be found. Long before 1782, however, the scholarship had departed from Berkeley's expectations. Most Berkeley scholars resided only one year, not three; and the Bishop's land did not always produce enough income in rent to support three scholars.[12]

The Berkeley foundation comprised most—and perhaps all—of the gifts that Yale received for scholarships before 1800. Harvard received about forty such gifts in these years, but most of them were smaller than the Hopkins or Hollis foundations. By the middle of the eighteenth century, these smaller foundations were still aiding about fifteen scholars a year, excluding the Hopkins and Hollis scholars, though it is obvious from the amounts paid in 1750 that most exhibitions were failing to cover even the cost of tuition.[13] Moreover, all the exhibitions given in 1750 came from funds given to the college before 1737; one fund dated back to 1686, while the rest had been established after 1700. In other words, most of the aid that Harvard offered in 1750 came from gifts accumulated from donors in England in the early eighteenth century.[14]

Few traces of these early scholarships remained after the American Revolution. Catalogs that the colleges began to publish in the early nineteenth century—in part to inform the poor about financial aid—cited only a few old funds. Scholarships at Harvard and Yale, in most cases, were not replenished after 1750, either by additional gifts or through profits from investment.

Donations continued for buildings, books, and professorships, but those for scholarships did not. After 1740 the number of gifts endowing scholarships at Harvard declined and did not rise again until the middle of the nineteenth century. Most of those received before the nineteenth century were given between 1700 and 1738, a period of generous contribution. The list of donations compiled by Josiah Quincy for his 1840 *History of Harvard University* included eighteen gifts for exhibitions between 1700 and 1780; sixteen of these came in the early period, between 1700 and 1738, but only two small ones were added thereafter.[15] If Harvard received any other significant donations for scholarships after 1740, they had been forgotten by 1840. The Harvard treasurer's statement for that year names no fund that could have been received between 1740 and 1780; it lists one legacy of 1785, but all others were received before 1740 or after 1800. Harvard suffered a sixty-year drought.[16]

Yale probably received no major gifts for scholarships in the eighteenth century other than Berkeley's.[17] Ezra Stiles mentioned no other scholarships in his diary for the years of his presidency, 1778 to 1795. The diary makes it clear that in the late eighteenth century Yale wanted money to construct buildings, improve its library, and endow professorships, but Stiles did not look for scholarship endowments in his fund raising. He referred every year to "monitorships" and "waiterships," terms which indicate that the college did provide some work for poor students; but, almost as frequently, he made entries like the one for June 8, 1782, when a student named Welles, "an ingenious Scholar, an Orphan," requested a dismission, "his Circumstances as to Estate not permitting his finishing an academic Education."[18] Welles is not listed among Yale graduates.

Scholarships also declined because colleges had difficulty investing their funds, especially in colonial New England. English universities invested in land, but land was less valuable in America. Rents were hard to collect, as Harvard discovered with its Hopkinton lands, and they were low, as Yale discovered with Bishop Berkeley's farm. Land values rose slowly, if at all. Yale officials, complaining that short-term leases produced little income, "which is likely to be the Case for some Centuries while Land is so plenty in this

Country," finally leased the farm in 1762 for 999 years. Income decreased as the farm declined in condition, a fact which may explain why the college had trouble finding scholars to accept this grant from Berkeley.[19]

The Hopkins scholarships at Harvard suffered similarly. As Josiah Quincy explained in 1840, "Great losses and many obstructions, arising in later times from the nature of investment, prevented the Trustees from attaining by that donation all the advantages, which the original rents were calculated to yield."[20] The Hopkins fund managed to survive until the nineteenth century, making it a rarity among colonial scholarship foundations; by 1833 it had accumulated $18,000, and by 1840 it reached $30,000. Still, between 1727 and 1833 Harvard could add only one scholarship to the Hopkins list, making an insignificant seven in all when Benjamin Peirce wrote his history of the college. In most other cases, investments yielded a decreasing income for scholarships.[21]

Economic conditions undermined these funds, and the flow of gifts from England stopped. None of the provincial colleges founded after 1765 had endowments for scholarships.[22] In New England, therefore, the scholarship virtually disappeared, changing the material base of higher education, especially for the poor. By 1800 very different forms of student aid began to appear.

By the early nineteenth century, Harvard had gathered most of its separate little "exhibition funds" into a single, consolidated "beneficiary fund."[23] Other colleges were creating similar funds at this time, usually called "charity funds." In one respect, charity funds resembled the scholarships they replaced: they generally came from an endowment controlled by the college.[24] Those at Harvard were endowed with old exhibition funds. Amherst College put its entire initial endowment in 1821 into a charity fund, giving itself the character of a charity school. Yale created its first charity fund in the mid-1820s and added endowments to it after 1840.[25]

For those who received its meager aid, however, the charity fund provided only a pinched substitute for the scholarship. No honor attached to an allowance from such a fund; it was a dole and never lost the odium of a dole. It provided a fraction of its total worth to as many students as applied; it recognized need, not excellence. Its beneficiaries received no fixed stipend from endowments. They merely found themselves excused from paying charges borne by more affluent classmates. In some cases beneficiaries might receive small sums of money, clothing, food, furniture, or bedding, but in no way did the status and amount of their allowance compare favorably to that of an endowed scholarship.[26]

Nor did the charity fund provide the security of the old scholarship. No beneficiary of a charity fund could expect "sufficient maintenance" for full-time study, even through his first degree. If he were optimistic, a charity scholar might hope to have his tuition cancelled, leaving him to meet only his other expenses. At Amherst in 1839-40, a student could arrange to have thirty-three dollars tuition deducted from necessary expenses, estimated at $116.00 to $150.00. At Williams College in 1841-42 a charity student might expect a two-thirds remittance of his tuition by the college fund—or a twenty dollar deduction from necessary expenses, which ranged from $97.50 to

$142.00. Favors of comparable leanness could be expected at most New England colleges.[27]

The scale of college assistance in the period of the charity fund became more modest, therefore, than Jonathan Mitchell had imagined even for his day of "small things." The prevailing assumption was, in fact, that outside sources of aid would be necessary. Yale had two charity funds in 1841, when enrollment stood at 410 undergraduates. One fund of $1,000 was "appropriated to the relief of indigent students," probably in small emergency sums; a second, initiated in 1841, provided for the remission of full tuition for twenty students and partial tuition for thirty more. Perhaps sixty or seventy students were aided in these small ways. At Williams in the same year, the charity fund produced $800 in income and provided two-thirds tuition for perhaps forty of Williams's 144 students. Harvard's beneficiary fund produced about $1,400 for undergraduates through the 1840s, aiding perhaps thirty-five out of about 275 undergraduates. At Amherst, where the charity fund had been the original endowment of the college, $1,578.97 was remitted in the college bills of charity students in 1828; this sum could have covered tuition for about fifty students.[28] In these years the colleges no longer controlled the most important sources of support for poor students. The charity that they offered in the 1830s and 1840s was much less than the funds commanded by the national education societies, the largest agencies of student assistance. In 1835 the American Education Society alone disbursed $55,213 to 1,040 indigent scholars.[29]

Despite the considerable number of students who drew from them, charity funds were not greatly sought after, inadequate as they were for the demands of the early nineteenth century. Though they were still operating at the end of the century, they had been supplemented and largely replaced by other forms of aid within the colleges. In 1838 Harvard received its first endowment for a loan fund, and in 1848 the college began to transfer income from its beneficiary fund to the loan fund, explaining that "some students would prefer to receive the aid in the form of a loan." Yale, too, created a loan fund from payments by former charity students. But most institutions did not create loan funds until after 1900.[30]

By the late nineteenth century, all New England colleges had reinvented the scholarship, permitting them to assume once more the kind of patronage of poor scholars that they had abandoned to the education societies. Yale announced its first new scholarship in 1846, followed by Harvard in 1852, Amherst in 1858, and Williams in 1870. By 1889 Harvard was boasting in its catalog that "good scholars of high character but slender means are very rarely obliged to leave College for want of money."[31]

However, the situation in which this boast became possible developed only after the 1850s. Before that time, the only provisions, apart from charity, that colleges could make for poor students consisted of what little economies the schools might enforce to reduce the cost of higher education. They could shorten the time a student spent in school, foster arrangements for inexpensive food and housing, and encourage a poor scholar to find work outside the college to support himself, but they could not offer him a competent subsistence. For students, this loss of patronage—an ironic development in social history—meant hardship, but it also brought a new degree of independence, both from the material support of the colleges and from their control. For the colleges, a diminished role in patronage entailed a significant loss of power over the student population. That power fell at once to totally new kinds of organizations outside the colleges and to the students themselves.

Notes

1 Benjamin Peirce, *A History of Harvard University* (Cambridge, Mass.: Brown, Shattuck, and Company, 1833); Josiah Quincy, *The History of Harvard University*, 2 vols. (Cambridge, Mass.: John Owen, 1840); Samuel A. Eliot, *A Sketch of the History of Harvard College and of Its Present State* (Boston: Charles C. Little and James Brown, 1848).

2 Quoted in Samuel Eliot Morison, *Three Centuries of Harvard, 1636-1936* (Cambridge, Mass.: Harvard University Press, 1937), p. 295.

3 Beverly McAnear, "College Founding in the American Colonies, 1745-1775," *Mississippi Valley Historical Review* 42 (1955): 24-44. McAnear's research on eighteenth-century colleges also leads to this conclusion. The bulk of my evidence comes from college records and from information on scholarships in college catalogs of the nineteenth century. Modern historical studies of individual colleges also support this conclusion; see Seymour E. Harris, *Economics of Harvard* (New York: McGraw-Hill, 1970), pp. 85-105.

4 Wilbur K. Jordan has noted the same imprecision in sixteenth- and seventeenth-century English philanthropy. Jordan adopts the modern distinction between scholarships and fellowships in his discussion; he defines *scholarship* as "the funds supporting or helping to support a student in school, college, or university" and *fellowship* as "the status or emoluments of a graduate fellow, one of the teaching or voting members of a college or university." See Jordan, *Philanthropy in England, 1480-1660* (London: George Allen & Unwin Ltd., 1959), p. 291, n. 2. I am adopting Jordan's definition here, with certain differences. The idea of a scholarship implied more than acts of charity toward students, or remission of term bills—which are kinds of support; it implied a stipend sufficient to maintain a student with "competent & necessary subsistence," without forcing him to resort to other forms of charity or to forms of labor that might take him away from his studies, though this stipend need not provide complete support. I also restrict the term to those stipends paid annually from income

derived from endowment funds or from annual subscriptions. See also Philippe Aries, *Centuries of Childhood: A Social History of Family Life*, trans. Robert Baldick (New York: Alfred A. Knopf, 1962), pp. 155-58.

5 Samuel Eliot Morison, ed., *Harvard College Records*, Publications of the Colonial Society of Massachusetts (Boston, 1935), 3: 316-17, 321.

6 Ibid., pp. 315-22.

7 Jordan, *Philanthropy in England*, pp. 292-94; Wilbur K. Jordan, *The Charities of London, 1480-1660* (London: George Allen & Unwin Ltd., 1960), pp. 52-53, 58-59, 169, 171-72.

8 Albert Matthews, ed., *Harvard College Records*, Publications of the Colonial Society of Massachusetts (Boston, 1925), 2: 836-37 (hereafter cited as *Harvard Records*).

9 Quincy, *Harvard*, 1:237, 529, 530-31; "College Book IV," *Harvard Records*, 2:477. For an estimate of the cost of a year at Harvard through 1712, see Margery Somers Foster, *"Out of Smalle Beginnings . . .": An Economic History of Harvard College in the Puritan Period (1636 to 1712)* (Cambridge, Mass.: Harvard University Press, Belknap Press, 1962), pp. 74-75.

10 Daniel Coit Gilman, "Bishop Berkeley's Gifts to Yale College," *Papers of the New Haven Colony Historical Society* 1 (New Haven, 1865): 155-56.

11 "College Book IV," *Harvard Records*, 2:640, 701, 740-41, 772, 788, 804.

12 Ezra Stiles, *The Literary Diary of Ezra Stiles*, ed. Franklin B. Dexter, 3 vols. (New York: Charles Scribner's Sons, 1901), 3:20; see also Gilman, "Berkeley's Gifts," pp. 156-60.

13 "College Book IV," *Harvard Records*, 2:797-99, 816-17, 821-23.

14 Foster, *"Out of Smalle Beginnings,"* pp. 138-41, 206; Benjamin Wadsworth, "Benjamin Wadsworth's Book," *Harvard Records*, 3:491-92. Gifts can be dated by using the Harvard record books and the donation lists printed in Quincy, *Harvard*, 1:506-13; 2:525-31.

15 Quincy, *Harvard*, 2:525-31.

16 Ibid., 2:616-23, 629.

17 Donation lists compiled by President Clap cover 1700 to 1766; another list by Ebenezer Baldwin covers 1766 to 1831. Both are printed in Ebenezer Baldwin, *Annals of Yale College, in New Haven Connecticut, from Its Foundation, to the Year 1831* (New Haven: Hezekiah Howe, 1831), pp. 306-21.

18 Stiles, *Diary*, 3:8, 24, 382, 426, 465; 2:384-89.

19 Quoted in Henry Fuller, "Bishop Berkeley as a Benefactor of Yale," *Yale University Library Gazette* 28 (1953): 13-14. See also Foster, *"Out of Smalle Beginnings,"* pp. 156-57, for a discussion of problems of investment.

20 Quincy, *Harvard*, 1:205.

21 Peirce, *Harvard*, p. 104 and Appendix, p. 27; Quincy, *Harvard*, 1:170. Examples of disappearing funds are the Pennoyer, Mowlson, and Keayne funds at Harvard. See Samuel Eliot Morison, *Harvard College in the Seventeenth Century*, 2 vols. (Cambridge, Mass.: Harvard University Press, 1936), 2:378-89; Foster, *"Out of Smalle Beginnings,"* p. 110; Andrew M. Davis, "The First Scholarship at Harvard College," *Proceedings of the American Antiquarian Society*, n.s., 5 (1887): 139.

22 McAnear, "College Founding," pp. 39, 28-29.

23 In the treasurer's statement for 1840, this fund is referred to as an "exhibition" fund or as "funds for indigent students." It is the same fund that is cited in the printed Harvard catalogs as the "beneficiary fund," the term used by Quincy and Kirkland. Quincy, *Harvard*, 2:368, 561-62, 616-17, 629.

24 Sources for this discussion of the charity fund are the college catalogs published before 1860.

25 William S. Tyler, *History of Amherst College During Its First Half Century, 1821-1871* (Springfield, Mass.: Clark W. Bryan and Company, 1873), pp. 40-46; Stanley King, *A History of the Endowment of Amherst College* (Amherst, Mass.: Amherst College, 1950), pp. 10-23; *Catalogue of the Officers and Students in Yale College, 1841-42* (New Haven: B. L. Hamlen, 1841), p. 31.

26 For example, see *Catalogue of the Officers and Students of Amherst College, 1839-40* (Amherst, Mass.: J. S. & C. Adams, 1839), p. 24.

27 Ibid., p. 23; *Catalogue of the Corporation, Officers and Students of Williams College, 1841-42* (Troy, N.Y.: N. Tuttle, 1841), p. 19. Necessary expenses in most catalogs included tuition, room rent, board, fuel, light, washing, books, furniture, and bedding. They did not include board and room during vacation (about twelve weeks each year), clothing, travel, or pocket money.

28 *Catalogue of Yale, 1841-42*, p. 31; *Catalogue of Williams, 1841-42*, p. 19; *Catalogue of the Officers and Students of the University at Cambridge [Mass.], for the Academical Year, 1848-49*, 2d ed. (Cambridge, Mass.: Metcalf and Company, 1848), pp. 69-70; King, *Endowment of Amherst*, pp. 214-17.

29 *Fiftieth Annual Report of the Directors of the American Education Society* (Boston: T. R. Marvin, 1866), p. 11; *Nineteenth Annual Report of the Directors of the American Education Society* (Boston: Perkins, Marvin & Co., 1835), p. 55.

30 *Catalogue of [Harvard], 1848-49*, p. 69; *Catalogue of Yale University, 1889-90* (New Haven: Tuttle, Morehouse & Taylor, 1889), p. 64.

31 *Harvard University Catalogue, 1889-90* (Cambridge, Mass.: Harvard University, 1889), p. 150. Harvard offered 125 undergraduate scholarships in 1889, in addition to other forms of aid. Yale offered 50, Amherst more than 45, in addition to its charity funds; and Williams had 40 scholarship funds.

4 The Little
Education Societies

*From all parts of the land, the cry ascends, Give us Ministers, or we die;
and pious young men, smitten with compassion, spring up and rush to our
College, and offer themselves to the Lord, and no provision is made to
receive them.*

Lyman Beecher, 1814

All across New England and New York State between 1810 and 1820, small
associations began to form and to assume the charitable functions once performed only by individual churches and colleges. These little education
societies arose simultaneously in small groups of communities, helping local
youths who needed money for education but who had no access to charity.
The need for aid was widespread. Autonomous little societies appeared
everywhere, without central organization, like sparks from the Second Great
Awakening. They marked the beginning of an indigenous benevolent movement, evolving eventually into very large organizations as the influx of
impoverished scholars really got under way. They were not mere imports from
Britain, or copies of English benevolent societies. Both in their origins and
in their development, they responded to local, native needs. At the same time,
the structures of these societies evolved in ways that changed the character
of charity.

Little education societies began to fill an institutional vacuum throughout
New England, where young men willing to study were more numerous than
local charities could support. Ministers, in particular, became aware of this

vacuum and of the need for new arrangements to fill it. Their work made them familiar with the stark, unadorned configurations of many young lives. They learned about collective need on a scale transcending a single church or town. This was especially true of ministers whose churches experienced frequent revivals of religion and who themselves had known the difficulties of student life in New England.

Such a man was Samuel Wood, who struggled for education at Dartmouth, became a minister, and himself eventually formed a kind of education society. His own life reflected the conditions of the young men who later became his beneficiaries. Wood was born May 11, 1752, at Mansfield, Connecticut, a village about fifty miles northeast of New Haven. He was the eldest of the thirteen children of Joseph and Ellen Palmer Wood, "worthy and pious persons," according to Wood's biographer, "whose first desire in respect to their children was, that they might grow up in the fear and love of God."[1] When Samuel was in his fourteenth year, about 1766, his father moved the family from Connecticut to a wilderness area at Lebanon, New Hampshire, "with a view to accommodate his numerous children with land for settlement." This move solved the problem of crowding, but it ruined the son's hopes of becoming a minister, "for, as he was the eldest son, he saw that his father's dependence would be upon *him*, in clearing up the forest." It also removed the family far from Yale College and the schools and churches of Connecticut towns.[2]

Lebanon, New Hampshire, had no church and could have provided only the most primitive religious and educational privileges during the earliest years of the Woods' settlement there. The family's deprivation, like that experienced by early settlers in most frontier communities, helps to explain the increasing demand for ministers, especially educated ministers, in frontier towns. Samuel Wood received his religious instruction from his mother. His religious conversion came to him in isolation, at the death of a brother, but he could make no profession of faith because there was no church. Nor was there a teacher or a minister nearby to prepare him for college, even had the time and funds been available. In 1769 his prospects brightened with the establishment of Dartmouth College at Hanover, only six miles from his father's farm; shortly thereafter a church was formed at Lebanon.[3]

The Reverend Isaiah Potter changed the life of Samuel Wood, an indication of the importance of a minister to the young males of a New England town in the middle of the eighteenth century. Potter graduated from Yale in 1767 and became Lebanon's first minister in 1770. Shortly after arriving, he brought Samuel Wood into his church and revived his young parishioner's desire to enter the ministry. Perhaps because Wood was still helping clear land for the farm, it was not until four years later, when Wood had reached twenty-two, that Potter began to prepare his friend for college. In August 1775, Wood entered Dartmouth, "being then in his twenty-fourth year." He stayed for a full four-year course and was graduated in 1779, delivering a valedictory address on the "importance of education." Within seven weeks he had received his license to preach and had delivered his first sermon, at Lebanon.[4]

Like Mark Hopkins, Wood had started college late. He could not begin to prepare until Potter arrived, when Wood was eighteen; and even his preparation was delayed for several more years, presumably because it took that long for the Wood family to clear its land. Yet his work on the farm fails to explain the delay completely, for it seems unlikely that Samuel Wood could have gone to college at all had Dartmouth not appeared. Poverty slowed his progress: to attend college in Hanover, just six miles away, Wood had to borrow several hundred dollars, perhaps through the good offices of Potter.[5]

In 1781 Wood became pastor at Boscawen, New Hampshire, and the following year he witnessed a revival among his congregation that added between thirty and forty heads of families to the church. He remained in this church for more than half a century, during which time there were ten revivals. Following the custom of ministers before him, he fitted about 100 young men for college, of whom roughly fifty became ministers.[6] Childless, but with a church whose revivals brought in many young men eager to join the ministry, Wood began to lend the students money.

He lived to see himself celebrated as the "venerable patriarch" of Boscawen. In 1834 he was visited by John Ellis, an agent of the American Education Society, who described their conversation together in a letter to the society. Ellis reviewed Wood's long career, his revivals, his many converts and students, and his practice of loaning money.

> He said he once had an education society of his own, and that although he was several hundred dollars in debt when he left college, and had nothing to pay, yet he afterwards had, at one time, $1,500 *loaned out* to his young men *without interest*—who refunded it for the use of others in the same pursuit. *This* man entered college at the age of TWENTY-FOUR.[7]

Ministers continued to aid the young men of their churches in much the same way that Potter helped Wood and Wood helped his own students. This arrangement between individual ministers and the indigent young men of their churches survived at least until the Civil War. It continued to exist alongside the education societies, which came to serve as alternatives to, rather than as complete replacements for, the older customs.

Yet, as the experience of Samuel Wood indicates, by the early nineteenth century, ministers everywhere in New England were beginning to experiment with more elaborate charity schemes. Such experiments revealed a need for more formal organizations involving groups of ministers, churches, and towns and for institutions designed specifically to support the education of larger numbers of poor young men gathered from different localities. Thus, poor students moved beyond the domain of an individual minister in a single church and town.

One type of innovation appeared among Yankees outside New England and can be traced through the careers of men like George Washington Gale, a minister in northern New York State. Gale ended his settlement at the church in Adams, New York, in 1824—pleading the common excuse of ill health—and retired to a farm near Western, New York, in Oneida County.

Here he devoted himself exclusively to the education of young men preparing for college.

Gale began his experiment with a class of six students, all of whom prepared for college on his farm. "He agreed to board and instruct them free of expense provided they would labour for him in the field, three hours every day," according to an account by the secretary of the American Education Society, who maintained a close interest in such projects. "Mr. Gale estimated the value of each young man's labour, at the close of the season, to be fifty dollars, which prevented him from sustaining any loss."[8] By 1827 Gale was describing this kind of arrangement as a "manual labor academy" and stressing its effect upon the health as well as the finances of indigent students. In 1827, in concert with other ministers and residents of Oneida County, Gale moved his experiment to Whitesboro and founded the Oneida Institute, employing the manual-labor plan on a larger scale and providing a more formal curriculum, calendar, and faculty. Ten years later he extended this innovation into still another form of institution, when he founded one of the many manual-labor colleges in the West.[9]

Institutions such as those devised by Gale were actually schools, providing as they did their own buildings, instruction, room, board, and sometimes clothing for indigent students. They were associated, for a brief time in the 1830s and 1840s, with the manual-labor movement, especially in the West. These institutions could be logically described as descendants of the kind of education society conducted by Samuel Wood at Boscawen, since they represented attempts to combine subsidized instruction with self-help in one semischolastic institution. Wood and Gale focused on the same problem: how to provide education for a particular group of students in a given community. Their methods differed significantly, however. Wood did no more than prepare his young church members for college, and his average number of scholars—about two per year—was much lower than Gale's average group. When he spoke of his "education society," Wood referred specifically to his loaning of money to poor boys, not to his teaching or preparing.

This distinction most clearly sets apart institutions offering instruction, like Gale's, from those properly called education societies, though nineteenth-century men often confused these new structures. Both sought to aid the indigent, but the local education societies, rather than providing instruction, specialized in benevolent support, the other half of Samuel Wood's function at Boscawen. Society funds might still be offered to young men from a specific group of towns, or to students at a particular college, but even those education societies that channeled their aid to a single college did not assume a teaching role, nor did they help start new schools. Moreover, nearly all education societies devoted themselves to a problem much broader than the education of students: perhaps because of their connection with the churches of New England, they shared a concern for providing educated, evangelical ministers to churches in destitute places.[10]

The little societies began to appear around 1810 in a form distinguishable from Samuel Wood's personal education society at Boscawen simply by the numbers of persons involved. The societies had to draw up constitutions, publish annual reports, and devise rules for beneficiaries and methods for raising funds—the trappings of early bureaucracy. Ministers, acting together, organized most of these societies out of small groups of churches, but in some cases church members, including the young men themselves, provided the impetus. The creation of the societies brought a formal structure to local arrangements for aiding indigent students and extended that aid to young men living in places unblessed by the benevolent presence of ministers like Samuel Wood.

The societies appeared suddenly, everywhere—especially, but not exclusively, in New England and New York—and among all evangelical denominations. The directors of the American Education Society later gathered documents on this movement.

> Little organizations and combinations of a local character were forming here and there, to assist young men on their way to the ministry. It is one of the best evidences that the impulse was from God, and was in harmony with the wants of the world, that Christians, in different places, and without consultation, were reaching out in their own way to compass this end.[11]

These "wants of the world" were the object of widespread, indigenous concern.

The directors of the national education societies that were to rise later in Boston, New York, and Philadelphia by no means created this concern. The grandeur of the American and Presbyterian education societies, as they organized their national operations after 1816, has obscured the little societies already growing from local impulses. Perhaps as early as 1809 there existed in Connecticut the Charitable Society in the North Consociation of Litchfield County, which drew its funds from the county's female charitable societies and used their members as agents to collect donations.[12] In 1813 the Benevolent Education Society was formed in Plymouth, Bristol, and Barnstable counties in Massachusetts. This group loaned money without interest; it became an auxiliary of the American Education Society in 1829.[13] Some of these local groups were absorbed into the national societies as auxiliaries; some disbanded; but a few maintained a separate existence, taking their places as living antiques alongside older arrangements like Samuel Wood's.

The earliest local society for whose founding a detailed account survives happens to be the one organized in Worcester County, Massachusetts, in 1812 by the Reverend Benjamin Wood, younger brother of Samuel. This account, appearing in a letter published by the American Education Society in 1866, was written sometime in 1865 or 1866 by "an aged gentleman," Deacon William Slocomb of Rochester, New York, who as a young man had lived in Sutton, Massachusetts, when the Religious Charitable Society for the County of Worcester was formed.[14] (By that date, no one had any reason to recall the relationship between Benjamin Wood of Upton and Samuel Wood of Boscawen.) Slocomb's letter and the record book of the Worcester County society make it possible to draw certain comparisons between the experiences of the Wood brothers in connection with education societies; they also suggest how the Worcester society was formed and what it intended to accomplish.

Benjamin Wood, almost a generation younger than his brother Samuel, was born at Lebanon, New Hampshire, in 1772. He was fitted for college by Samuel and graduated from Dartmouth at age twenty-one. In 1796 he was ordained pastor at Upton, in Worcester County, at the age of twenty-four. By 1812 he was forty years old and the father of a growing family that finally numbered seven children.[15] Unlike his childless brother, he could not have supported his own education society, though his church had promising young men. Instead, he agreed to embark on a collective venture with at least six other ministers in neighboring towns.[16]

Slocomb claimed that he had first proposed the idea for the Religious Charitable Society at the close of a prayer meeting in January 1812. His own minister consulted with Wood and others on the proposal of "forming a society for aiding young men of piety and talent in acquiring an education for the ministry," but they hesitated to take up the idea at that time. Among the hesitant was Benjamin Wood, though he figured in the founding five months later by preaching the sermon at the society's organizational meeting. By the time of the next meeting, Wood had put aside all caution about this novelty and had assumed the duties of secretary; all the early records of the society, therefore, are in his hand.[17]

The Worcester County society performed the functions of the old church charity funds, which many New England churches traditionally had maintained; in this case, the fund was raised collectively, rather than individually, by a group of rather poor congregations. At various times the society loaned or gave money to individuals and sought out poor young men in the county who merited financial aid to obtain a college education. Hopefully, these young men would settle in poor churches in Worcester County. The society's relations with its beneficiaries preserved the intimacy with which individual churches had supervised young men supported by their charity funds. The society watched the expenses of each student (a beneficiary could not even buy books without permission), determined where he should study, and scrutinized his theology. If he strayed from orthodoxy he had to pay back the money.[18]

Besides supporting its own indigent youth, the Worcester County society wanted to help "feeble churches and foreign missions" everywhere, a commitment that led to something more than a local enterprise.[19] The full implications of this broader commitment can be seen most clearly in the history of another organization; this was the Connecticut Education Society (or the Charitable Society for the Education of Indigent Pious Young Men for the Ministry of the Gospel, as it was first called), founded in 1814 with an appeal for funds by Lyman Beecher. At first, the C.E.S. appeared to function like the Worcester County society, but its peculiar problems and new measures gave it a different character. It was, in fact, the embryo of a new institution.

The Connecticut Education Society probably evolved from the earlier charity group in Litchfield County, where Beecher was settled. Its constitution scaled everything to the local level, fixing small dues and making concessions to local desires. Article Ten gave first preference for aid to descendants of life members and second preference to descendants of persons giving more than twenty dollars. Article Fourteen permitted donors of $100 to nominate their own beneficiaries.[20]

Provisions like these permitted ministers to select boys in their own congregations and support them with money from the society. Nathaniel Bouton, an indentured apprentice until he was seventeen, was able to enter Yale in 1818 at the age of nineteen when four ministers of Darien, New Canaan, and Wilton agreed to pay at least $100 to the society.[21] Thus, the C.E.S. preserved a vestige of the relationship between patron and beneficiary that had characterized the Worcester County society and all earlier forms of charity.

And like the Worcester and Litchfield societies, the C.E.S. was composed of ministers—but they came not merely from small clusters of neighboring congregations but also from 200 churches all over Connecticut. They performed only small, specialized tasks, working "within their respective limits, particularly by soliciting subscriptions and donations, and by encouraging the formation of auxiliary societies." In other words, they acted as ordinary agents in a nascent bureaucratic structure, centralizing at Yale College. Key positions went to Yale faculty members; annual meetings took place in New Haven, after commencement. The treasurer of the C.E.S. was also treasurer of the college, and Yale professors comprised its Committee of Appropriations, governing the selection of "objects of charity."[22] These operations passed beyond the local level. In scope and structure, the Connecticut Education Society foreshadowed a new kind of organization, different from the county societies.

Founders of the New Haven society only appeared to be responding to a local situation when they announced their intention "to furnish pecuniary assistance to indigent young men of piety and promising talents, intended for the ministry of the Gospel, in obtaining an education at Yale College."[23] Although only the college at New Haven was involved, by 1814 Yale was not, strictly speaking, a local institution. Yale found itself trying to accommodate "indigent young men of piety and promising talents" not merely from New Haven and the Connecticut River Valley—they came from everywhere, and they threw themselves upon the charity of the college. Yale, too, was experiencing an influx of poor students.

Lyman Beecher described the situation created by the arrival of these poor and pious boys in his appeal of 1814.

> For a number of years past, from 16 to 20 applications of this kind have been made and refused. There are at this time several young men in Yale College who, hearing that this society had been organized, have come and flung themselves upon us. We could not send them away, and yet, unless we are patronized by the public, they must go away despairing of their object; for they stand in need of every thing, while as yet it is comparatively nothing that we can do.[24]

They converged on Yale from all directions, but especially from the north and west. Asa Turner arrived in the fall of 1823 from Worcester County, where he had been born in 1799. "I was an entire stranger and had never seen any one in college," he recalled. "My father carried me there in his buggy, gave me a bed and bedding and ten dollars. This was the amount of his contribution to my education." Until he was twenty-one, Asa had given all his earnings as a schoolteacher to his father. He boarded cheaply and during his second year taught school at Guilford. "The college woodyard opened the way to earn a little, by sawing wood." He depended entirely upon himself and the charity of the college.[25]

After Turner graduated in 1827, he walked home and back—240 miles—to bring his younger brother Jonathan to Yale. Their father wanted Jonathan to stay home and had given him the farm when he turned twenty-one. Asa persuaded the old man to let Jonathan enter Yale instead, at twenty-two. The Turner family of Worcester County thus sent two indigent sons to Yale.[26]

Beecher wanted to accommodate as many as 100 of these students annually in the college, with funds gathered from Connecticut churches, Yale alumni, and wealthy individuals. He knew that their presence would change the character of the college.[27] At one point in the eighteenth century, in fact, Yale had tried to prohibit young men over twenty-one from entering its freshman class. This prohibition, enacted in 1744 during the first Great Awakening, probably was aimed at mature religious enthusiasts rather than at the poor; had it been enforced in the early nineteenth century, students like the Turners could not have enrolled.[28]

By this time, however, Beecher was able to justify aid to the indigent on the grounds of their religiosity. He clearly assumed that these indigent students came from a different social order and differed greatly in character and temperament from the ordinary Yale boy. This was all to the good. "What a security to our sons," said Beecher, the son of a blacksmith, "to have in the College, whither we send them, a select band of pious companions to watch over and pray for them, and lead them in the right way." Under their pious influence, the college would become a place of revivals, where young men of all social classes would come for conversion.[29]

Beecher attributed the arrival of poor and pious young men at Yale College to the spreading of revivals among the middle classes and "downward to the cottage of the poor." In these classes the "great mass of talent, and piety, and zeal, and hardy enterprise" now resided. Young men without resources, but burning to preach the gospel, rushed to "our College" to offer themselves to the Lord.[30] With as much accuracy, Beecher might also have attributed their arrival to the *spreading* of the middle and lower classes; for in addition to revivals, these classes experienced a common migration to the West, where ministers who could prepare a young man for college and offer to support him were scarce, and where colleges were even more scarce. This had been the experience of Samuel Wood, whose father moved his family from Mansfield, Connecticut, in 1766. It was also the experience of the famous evangelist Charles Grandison Finney, whose father moved to Oneida County, New York, from Warren, Connecticut, in 1794, and of Julian Sturtevant, whose father moved from the same Connecticut town in 1816.

Sturtevant was born at Warren in 1805. When he was eleven, his parents moved to Tallmadge, Ohio, where they duplicated the experience of the Wood family in New Hampshire, including the gathering of a church. In 1822, when Sturtevant was almost seventeen and his brother nineteen, they joined a neighbor boy, Elizur Wright, Jr., in a plan to return to Connecticut and enroll at Yale College. (Finney made a similar pilgrimage at the age of twenty, though he decided not to enroll.) They had only a small income from their beehives; their horse, the gift of a local minister, was all he could give them.

> It may appear strange that our parents should consent that two sons . . . should try their fortunes at Yale with absolutely no resources to depend upon. It was a venture which nothing could excuse but their firm trust in Providence. It must be remembered that we had a grandmother and an uncle and aunt living only forty miles from New Haven to whom we could go in case of necessity.[31]

Sturtevant was accommodated at Yale, receiving special consideration because he was poor. He ate in the dining hall and attended classes on the understanding that he would pay what he could and give his note for the rest—without security. Several times he found his term bills paid by an anonymous source. "Our venerable mother Yale, had some peculiar ways in dealing with her numerous family of boys." He also received assistance from the American Education Society: "My college course would scarcely have been possible without it."[32]

By the time that Sturtevant enrolled at Yale, the little society for which Beecher was pleading in 1814 had been superseded by the American Education Society. In fact, Beecher had cast his appeal for the Connecticut Education Society in terms that implied that even a statewide group aiding students at a single college could not cope with educational needs arising from social change throughout New England and the West. He spoke of raising an army of ministers to supply churches in desolate areas like those settled by the Wood and Sturtevant families. He implied even as he gave his address in 1814 that the organization must give way to a much larger structure, with methods more innovative than those of the little education societies. The time had passed when the population of poor students could be supported through the charity structure of local communities; student society of the nineteenth century demanded something on a newer and grander scale.

Notes

1 William B. Sprague, *Annals of the American Pulpit*, 7 vols. (New York: Robert Carter & Brothers, 1859), 2:169.
2 Ibid., p. 169.
3 Ibid., pp. 169-70.
4 Ibid., p. 170.
5 "Rev. Mr. Ellis's Report," *American Quarterly Register* 7 (1834): 83.
6 Sprague, *Annals*, 2:170-71. Ellis estimated

that twelve revivals had taken place in Wood's church and that forty ministers had been fitted for college by Wood.
7 "Ellis's Report," p. 83.
8 Elias Cornelius, "Union of Study with Useful Labour," *American Quarterly Register* 2 (1829): 65.
9 William L. Raub, "Gale, George Washington," *Dictionary of American Biography*,

eds. Allen Johnson and Dumas Malone, vol. 7 (New York: Charles Scribner's Sons, 1931), p. 99.

10 For lists of these societies, see Charles I. Foster, *An Errand of Mercy: The Evangelical United Front, 1790-1837* (Chapel Hill: University of North Carolina Press, 1960), pp. 275-79; "Education Societies," *American Quarterly Register* 2 (1829): 35-36; William Cogswell, *Letters to Young Men Preparing for the Christian Ministry* (Boston: Perkins & Marvin, 1837), pp. 226-27; *Eighth Annual Report of the American Education Society* (Andover, Mass.: Flagg and Gould, 1823), pp. 45-47.

The Congregational Library in Boston has in its collections the manuscript records of two local societies, together with many published annual reports of local societies throughout New England. The Forbes Library in Northampton, Massachusetts, has the manuscript records of the Hampshire Education Society. All these documents indicate the important role of ministers like the Wood brothers in organizing and supervising local societies. The lists of beneficiaries that appear in some records and reports indicate that charity from these societies went exclusively to young men from local towns, or in some cases to students in local colleges.

11 *Fiftieth Annual Report of the Directors of the American Education Society* (Boston: T. R. Marvin, 1866), p. 6.

12 James Beach to the Editors, *Connecticut Evangelical Magazine* 8 (1815): 194.

13 "Education Societies," pp. 35-36.

14 *Fiftieth Report of the A.E.S.*, p. 7.

15 Sprague, *Annals*, 2:172.

16 *Fiftieth Report of the A.E.S.*, pp. 6-8.

17 Record Book of the Religious Charitable Society in the County of Worcester, Massachusetts, May 20, 1812, American Education Society Archives, Congregational Library, Boston, Mass.

18 Ibid., April 20, 1814, April 19, 1815, April 25, 1820, April 24, 1822, April 30, 1823, April 25, 1827, September 16, 1829, and September 22, 1831.

19 *Fiftieth Report of the A.E.S.*, p. 8.

20 [Lyman Beecher], *An Address of the Charitable Society for the Education of Indigent Pious Young Men, for the Ministry of the Gospel* (n.p., [1814]), pp. 26-27.

21 Nathaniel Bouton, *Autobiography of Nathaniel Bouton* (New York: Anson D. F. Randolph & Company, 1879), pp. 16, 20.

22 [Beecher], *Address*, pp. 26-28.

23 Ibid., p. 25.

24 Ibid., p. 23.

25 George F. Magoun, *Asa Turner: A Home Missionary Patriarch and His Times* (Boston: Congregational Sunday-School and Publishing Society, [1889]), pp. 16, 45-46.

26 Mary Turner Carriel, *The Life of Jonathan Baldwin Turner* (n.p., 1911), p. 6.

27 [Beecher], *Address*, pp. 15-18.

28 Franklin B. Dexter, ed., *Documentary History of Yale University* (New Haven: Yale University Press, 1916), pp. 365-66.

29 [Beecher], *Address*, pp. 21-22.

30 Ibid., pp. 14, 22-23.

31 Julian Sturtevant, *Julian M. Sturtevant: An Autobiography*, ed. J. M. Sturtevant, Jr. (New York: F. H. Revell Company, [1896]), pp. 14, 40, 68-69, 70.

32 Ibid., pp. 79-81.

5 The Strangeness of the American Education Society

We had long noticed things in the arrangements of the American Education Society which seemed strange and novel; but so full was our persuasion of the importance of the sacred cause, in which it was laboring, that we did not dare permit ourselves to think there was any error.

James Carnahan, 1829

The pattern of educational charity changed after 1815 with the rise of the American Education Society. A prodigy of size and organization, the A.E.S. made it impossible to think of student aid in eighteenth-century terms. Before 1815, when the poor had depended on wealthy individuals and small churches for funds, the very scale of patronage had fostered a powerful, familial image: patrons, churches, and even the little education societies all "adopted" their beneficiaries and assumed an intimate, paternal watchfulness over them.

After 1815 indigent students no longer depended solely upon small sources of charity in their own communities. No longer did they have to endure the paternalism of older charities, for they could turn instead to an institution too large to function like a family. As the number of A.E.S. beneficiaries climbed toward 1,000, totally new arrangements for student aid appeared, transforming the situation of indigent students in the nineteenth century and creating an organization of unprecedented size and influence over the student population.

The American Education Society began on a modest scale, differing only imperceptibly from older forms of patronage or from the workings of other little charitable societies. The prominent ministers and volunteers who founded the society at Boston in the summer of 1815 supported no more than seven beneficiaries in their first year, on funds they raised almost entirely in the Boston area. Their first subscriptions amounted to only $5,000, from which they appropriated less than $500.[1] Yet these men clearly had more grandiose projects in mind. By 1819 they were aiding 161 students all over New England, and during the next twenty years they saw the number of their beneficiaries spiral dramatically upward. In 1829 that number reached 404—more students than were enrolled at any single institution of higher education in America. The peak came in 1838, when 1,141 received A.E.S. assistance. Half of these were enrolled in colleges; most of them were in New England, where one college student in every seven was a beneficiary of the American Education Society.[2] People began to describe these students in military metaphors: the A.E.S. had raised an army.

This transformation in the scale of student aid can be attributed, in one sense, simply to the design of the A.E.S. founders and directors—to the scope of their ambitions. These men actively sought beneficiaries in numbers that made change necessary. Their motives were orthodox. As ministers and members of Congregational churches, fearing Catholic expansion in America, they hoped to find enough young men from lower-class Protestant families to fill an increasing number of vacant pulpits. At the same time, sensing the competition from Methodist and Baptist ministries, the A.E.S. founders intended to preserve collegiate education as a professional standard in the ministry, eliminating the "various ways which are open to young men, of getting into the ministry, without a regular course of classical study." They committed themselves to the old notion of the minister as a settled pastor over a thousand souls, whose education gave him "that power which is always the prerogative of superior attainments."[3]

Since migrations to the West had created a demand for educated ministers in the Mississippi Valley as well as in New England, the A.E.S. founders confronted a demographic problem of immense proportions. They were responding to the same social and demographic changes that were prompting other men to devise innovations in the structure of American political parties, newspapers and communications, manufacturing, banking, and business. Like the abolitionists, the revivalists, and the innovators in business organization (like the Tappans of New York), they, too, were reaching out for a new form of organization, creating the precursor of a classic, Weberian bureaucracy. They were involved in a paradox. Dedicated to preserving local worlds ruled by prominent men and ministers of superior attainments, they invented a machine that trampled on traditional ties between fathers and sons, families and churches, superiors and inferiors. In trying to save a remnant of the traditional village, they reared a bureaucracy that intruded into hundreds of communities and offered local youth an avenue of flight. Eventually, persons with conventional minds detected the paradox and saw in the A.E.S. only strangeness, novelty, and error.[4]

From the start, the directors knew that their old-fashioned commitment to a traditional ministry must involve them in creating a large institution. Eleazar Lord, who composed a prospectus for the A.E.S. in 1814, complained that nothing was being done by the church to recruit young men "on such a scale as to promise to remedy the evil." Local efforts were feeble. If the church were to find enough young men to fill vacant pulpits in New England and the Mississippi Valley, it would have to take measures "which have never been required before."[5] Recruiting indigent young men for the beneficiary lists of the A.E.S. began within three years of Lord's appeal. Within fifteen years, A.E.S. directors were vowing to support "every young man of proper character in the United States, who may apply for aid, and who may not be otherwise provided for." Late in 1828, the society's new secretary, Elias Cornelius, declared a goal of 4,000 beneficiaries—a total nearly equal to the entire college student population of the United States at that time.[6] The magnitude of this commitment vastly stimulated the growth of the A.E.S.

Yet something other than the recruitment program was causing the number of applicants to rise. Revivals of religion after 1790 generated a desire among increasing numbers of indigent youth for careers in the ministry. The directors discovered that most of their first applicants in 1816 and 1817 were seeking aid after very recent religious experiences. The minutes of forty-eight early interviews survive in which the directors ascertained the religious history of forty applicants. Of these forty young men, only eight had been professed Christians for three years or longer; twenty-four had "professed religion" within the previous three years, fifteen of them within the previous year. Eight had not yet made formal professions of faith in established churches. A.E.S. agents learned to regard revivals as the major source of potential beneficiaries, especially in newly settled areas of the West and in New England hill towns. In the course of conducting fund-raising meetings, these agents occasionally found themselves confronting audiences who could offer more men than money.[7] In towns like Southampton, Massachusetts, local population pressures were causing the ranks of beneficiaries to swell.

The demand for aid on the part of growing numbers of indigent students simply overwhelmed all charitable arrangements that functioned at the local level, through the resources of a single church or town. Most new churches had no funds at all to offer young members who might want education. The pressures on local institutions had increased, moreover, because scholarships and exhibition funds had virtually disappeared, closing one important source of patronage altogether. Letters from beneficiaries of the American Education Society suggest that, for hundreds of poor students each year, sources of local assistance had run dry. "This is my only resource," wrote David Cushman of Bowdoin College in 1830, "and if I do not obtain assistance I shall be unable to become a minister and the course of my future life must be wholly different from what I think my real desires would have it." Students like David Cushman deluged the American Education Society with requests for aid. Twenty years after Lord's first appeal, the directors were pleading with young men not to inquire by letter about their applications; all applications, the 1833 report said, probably would be successful. By this time, then, the vow to assist all volunteers had become a way of coping with the number of inquiries.[8] And the A.E.S. was by no means receiving the entire volume of applications from indigent students. The Board of Education of the General Assembly of the Presbyterian Church supported about half as many students as the A.E.S. through the 1830s, and the Northern Baptist Education Society about one-tenth.[9]

The rise of this bureaucratic structure resulted from growth in the numbers of indigent students. Without those numbers, the A.E.S. would not have had to organize on a scale transcending local communities and isolated colleges. An abundance of poor students created the demographic precondition for such an institution, even though the A.E.S. itself began to contribute to that abundance. The American Education Society was an artifact of infiltration by the poor.

Virtually all the novelties in student patronage devised by the A.E.S. between 1815 and 1830 resulted simply from its immense growth, from the pressures of selecting, supervising, and supporting indigent students whose numbers always increased more readily than the sources of funds to support them. Had the A.E.S. continued to function on a small scale, its directors would not have had to abandon the old method of administering student charity at the community level, nor would they have had to rear a bureaucratic organization without precedent in American higher education. At first they assumed that the society would function in the manner of older, local charitable institutions, which it would then use to select, supervise, and help support its beneficiaries with the same paternal care traditionally associated with student charity. They discovered, however, that the social functions of small groups in isolated communities could not be assumed by a central institution as large as the A.E.S. without significant changes. They found themselves on unfamiliar ground, violating ancient customs, creating an entirely new kind of institution. At every turn, they were gathering old, local powers into their own hands.

Under the pressure of numbers, the power to select beneficiaries passed rapidly from local churches and schools into the hands of the society itself. The founders had feared that recruits might be difficult to find and had appealed at first to individual churches, schools, and families to offer promising candidates for patronage. These candidates were to be interviewed, in turn, by the directors themselves. As early as 1819, however, flaws had appeared in these arrangements, and a search had begun for new ways to select beneficiaries. The society announced that, despite appeals "in many places," it was refusing any longer to assign specific beneficiaries "as the particular objects of the charity of individual churches or benefactors." The burden of keeping records on all these details prohibited this concession to local institutions.[10] And it became apparent at once that the directors themselves could not interview and select all beneficiaries.

By 1826 the A.E.S. had discovered the need for a full-time professional staff to raise funds and process applications; a voluntary association of notable persons meeting four times a year could no longer manage the American Education Society as an avocation. "By general consent the time has come, when important charitable institutions must be managed by competent men, who shall be devoted to them as their business for life."[11] Elias Cornelius, a Salem minister who became secretary of the A.E.S. in 1826, moved the society's offices from their original location in Andover to Boston, where the greater concentration of business services might facilitate daily work. He hired part-time clerks, full-time agents, and a full-time assistant, since the task of keeping records and processing applications soon became "too arduous to be performed by one man." Even this staff was taxed by the volume of inquiries and applications. Cornelius's new assistant, Bela Bates Edwards, reflected on the mounting tasks: "*Eighty new* beneficiaries were received on the funds, at the quarterly meeting in Boston week before last," he wrote in his diary in October 1828. "It has made, of course, a great accession to our business."[12]

As business expanded, the duty of selecting beneficiaries finally fell to special examining boards scattered across the northern United States. These boards met at quarterly intervals, usually in college buildings, to interview applicants. Though the men who sat on the boards were local citizens, ministers, and college officials, this did not mean that they could choose beneficiaries in the old way, on the basis of intimate acquaintance and years of familiarity; most applicants came to them as total strangers. Nor did these boards exercise any real local control. As the need for efficiency increased, A.E.S. officials developed a set of abstract criteria that actually governed the process of selection, leaving little room for a local examiner to exercise his own judgment. If a young man could prove that he had pursued studies for a few months, he had talent; if he could demonstrate that he had been a professor of religion for six months, he was pious; if he pledged himself to a thorough course of theological education and if his references revealed no misbehavior, he had dedication and good character. Prominent persons from a young man's community simply provided testimonials that he met certain criteria; the decision to assist a student no longer came from those who knew him best. Abstract rules, not local personages, determined selection.[13]

Local personages also lost the power to supervise individual students in this army of young men whose gathering changed the whole relationship between patron and beneficiary. A.E.S. beneficiaries were too numerous and scattered to be watched closely, so they experienced very little of the paternal scrutiny that had accompanied earlier forms of charity. Their "escape" came as a surprise to the directors, who had appealed to ministers, teachers, and parents to watch over the young men. As early as July 1816, however, the directors were sensing the need for special "counsellors" to supervise beneficiaries at distant places.[14] But busy ministers could not observe the behavior, the budgets, or the religious habits of highly mobile students at distant schools. And although instructors might have watched each beneficiary quite closely, a teacher's self-interest could diminish the value of his inspection—especially at small schools where A.E.S. students provided crucial revenues. Complaints arose about the remoteness of the A.E.S., whose donors could gather no evidence of the talents, piety, and conduct of their anonymous scholars. Even during its peak years in the 1830s, the society seldom dismissed as many as ten students, for any reason.[15] The anxiety that this lapse created among A.E.S. officials can be gauged by the measures they devised to control their own students in as direct a fashion as possible. None of these measures worked in familiar ways, however, or restored the intimacy of the old arrangements at the local level.

Elias Cornelius tried to take this duty himself, resolving to maintain a personal, "pastoral supervision" when he became secretary in 1826, bringing with him the experience of his Salem pastorate. He would, he said, visit each school regularly, interviewing the young men and their instructors. He would become the "personal friend, and Pastor" of each beneficiary; he would watch the progress and behavior of all the beneficiaries and "stir up their minds to the duty of seeking a more ardent and devoted piety." Cornelius and his successor, William Cogswell, found it impossible to visit all schools, so they began to delegate this duty to other staff members. The accounts of Bela Bates Edwards's inspections at Yale and Amherst in 1832 suggest that none of these visitors ever became the personal friend and pastor of many beneficiaries. Edwards, who was assistant secretary, spent two days at Yale, meeting briefly with two-thirds of the society's young men and questioning college officers. At Amherst he interviewed college officials, saw about thirty-five beneficiaries individually, and addressed the whole group—in about the same length of time. Entire seasons and years might elapse between such visits. Cornelius's plan was abandoned within a few years. "The great obstacle to the full performance of this service," the society explained in 1835, "is, that the students are at more than a hundred and fifty different Institutions, spread over the whole country, some of them thousands of miles apart." An official would travel more than 15,000 miles a year—at a rate of fifty miles a day—to reach all these places, and then he would not be able to interview all beneficiaries. Geography alone prevented the application of Cornelius's model of pastoral supervision.[16]

"Pastoral letters" replaced pastoral visits. Cornelius addressed his first pastoral letter to a group of beneficiaries in 1827, offering the advice, instruction, and exhortation he might have given had he been able to meet each student in person. The pastoral letters of Secretary William Cogswell evolved into printed circulars and appeared together in 1837 as a student manual, "a friendly companion" entitled *Letters to Young Men Preparing for the Christian Ministry*, whose advice each student could follow at his own option.[17]

Eventually, the only forms of supervision employed by the A.E.S. were those that beneficiaries could exercise themselves. Each quarter, the presiding member of the beneficiaries' concert of prayer submitted a form letter affirming that a prayer meeting had been held, reporting absences, and describing the health of the students. In effect, students had begun to oversee their own religious habits.

To control the expenses of beneficiaries, the directors began as early as 1822 to employ a uniform "schedule," which students filled out themselves and submitted each quarter. At one time, beneficiaries had simply written personal letters whenever they needed money, according to the custom of many local charitable institutions; these letters, "sometimes illegible and often inaccurate and tedious," required "much patient study from the Clerk." The schedule evolved into a printed form on which all beneficiaries at each school reported how much each had spent and earned during the previous three months. In the long, neat rows of figures, directors could discover "at a glance" how many weeks the beneficiaries had studied; the prices and total amounts each had paid for board; the amounts spent for tuition, washing, room, fuel, lights, books, stationery, and incidental expenses; the debts of each young man; his receipts of money, books, or clothing; and the number of weeks each beneficiary had taught school, together with an accounting of any other kind of labor.[18] The society now possessed, in other words, an unequaled amount of information about student life in different sections of the country. The role of local inspectors had been reduced to the simple signing of a schedule.

Officials of the American Education Society resorted to these impersonal procedures of selection and supervision out of bureaucratic necessity—because they found their time consumed in raising money. The extension of aid to 100 students by the end of 1817 had forced the directors to cast about for contributions far beyond the Boston area, involving them in ever-increasing amounts of work. For the next twenty years, the society tried to invent methods of fund raising that would function automatically, freeing the secretary and his staff to supervise the beneficiaries. Although none of their new methods ever achieved this goal, they had one primary effect: they reduced the dependence of the A.E.S. upon contributions from local churches and charitable societies. That reduction involved a major transfer of power.

Even the original constitution of the society had envisioned a need for raising money outside the structure of established local institutions. It created a system of branch and auxiliary societies to gather funds for the parent society at Andover and Boston. Like other large benevolent societies, the A.E.S. organized fund-raising auxiliaries near home, chiefly in eastern Massachusetts; in areas distant from Boston, it organized branches—Maine, New Hampshire, Vermont, Connecticut, New York, Ohio, and Illinois. Branches enjoyed a small degree of autonomy: they could select their own beneficiaries and spend money raised in their areas, but they followed A.E.S. rules and had to send surplus funds to Boston. In fact, these societies proved incapable of supporting beneficiaries recruited within their own jurisdictions. Amateurs directed their affairs, and they had only local sources of charity. Since they continually drained the treasury of the parent society, by 1835 William Cogswell was ordering his agents to stop organizing local affiliates.[19]

As weaknesses in this system became apparent, the A.E.S. turned increasingly to professional agents who devoted their full time to soliciting funds. The society employed as many as six agents, who gathered donations door-to-door, at church meetings, and in revivals throughout the country. All four A.E.S. secretaries between 1826 and 1874 had experience in this kind of work. Yet even the agency system proved unreliable, too easily disrupted by the capriciousness of local generosity. Agents began to report scattered resentment of their activities in the early 1830s; the agency system never provided enough revenue to sustain the A.E.S., moreover, and, having ceased to hold any promise of expansion, it eventually fell into disuse.[20]

Branches, auxiliaries, and the agency system all retained a common flaw: they relied upon the benevolence of individual churches and communities. The experienced fund raisers who took control of the American Education Society in the late 1820s recognized this flaw and began to stress radical alternatives that would have gathered major sources of financial support entirely under the power of the A.E.S., freeing it from any ties to public opinion or patronage.

Between 1827 and 1835, the secretary and directors tried to accumulate a permanent investment fund. It was a shocking maneuver, given the existing prejudice against independent voluntary associations. Other benevolent societies, having less need than the A.E.S. for a constant, predictable income, had denied themselves this hoard. Popular criticism of the permanent fund, together with the financial demands of 1,000 beneficiaries, led the A.E.S. to abandon even this plan by the mid-1830s. The society was in a financial quandary.[21] Legacies could not provide secure income for the A.E.S. until the late 1840s, when the founding generation began to die. Confronted with quarterly demands that repeatedly exceeded income from all sources, the A.E.S. turned to the beneficiaries themselves.

The process of transforming beneficiaries into a source of revenue began unwittingly during the financial crisis of 1819, when a decline in donations nearly forced the directors to reduce the number of young men on their lists. To meet this emergency, they began to require each beneficiary to sign a note for half the amount that he received. In this way, the society could retain all its beneficiaries and then apply refunds to assist others. This measure remained in effect after the emergency had passed. When the directors decided in 1826 to require each beneficiary to sign notes for the full amount of his appropriation, the transformation was complete: assistance once extended "as an exclusive charity" became simply a loan.[22] Perhaps to ease doubts in their own minds, the directors adopted the term *parental loans* to describe this innovation.

The virtue of the loan arrangement lay in its promised ability to provide a permanent source of income that bore some relation to the number of students assisted. It might create a "common stock," which beneficiaries would replenish in growing amounts as their numbers increased. William Cogswell predicted that repayments would become the society's chief source of revenue, yielding an expected $20,000 annually from former beneficiaries alone.[23] Moreover, the repayment system promised to solve all the problems that had perplexed officials from the start—freeing them from the burdens of fund raising, since repayment proceeded automatically. These funds would fall exclusively within the society's control, having no connection whatsoever with the troublesome little charitable societies and churches whose charity had to be primed individually in so many different towns.

Innovations in the process of selecting beneficiaries, in supervising them, and in raising funds followed no models or precedents; they appeared naturally, as it seemed to the directors, in response to particular problems arising in the course of long experience.[24] Not until the society attempted to describe its new arrangements in the annual reports for 1826 and 1827 did the significance of the transformation begin to emerge. Then, for the first time, the bureaucratic structure, the schedules, and the loans began to appear as related parts of a single, grand system. Once all the reforms had been set forth in context, doubts arose which led to controversies that revealed the social changes implicit in the ambitious new arrangements.

Late in the summer of 1829, James Carnahan, the new president of the College of New Jersey, composed a long critique of the reforms announced at Boston. "We had long noticed things in the arrangements of the American Education Society which seemed strange and novel," Carnahan wrote; "but so full was our persuasion of the importance of the sacred cause, in which it was laboring, that we did not dare permit ourselves to think there was any error."[25] It took time for Carnahan to collect his doubts; now, two years after the *Eleventh Annual Report* of 1827, he published the criticisms that launched a series of debates about the A.E.S., the most revealing of which was between Professor Moses Stuart of Andover Theological Seminary and Carnahan himself.

Both men were particularly qualified for their roles in this controversy. Stuart had been among those prominent persons who first sensed the need for an A.E.S. in 1815, and for fifteen years had followed the growth of the society, many of whose officers lived in Andover and were his friends. Carnahan had become aware of the problems of indigent students through his own experience at Princeton. Before his term as president began in 1823, enrollment had declined from a peak of about 120 to around 70 students. Carnahan tried to revive the institution by encouraging inexpensive boarding and lodging for the pupils; eventually, he added to the college charity funds and raised new scholarships, creating a permanent source of support within the institution for poor scholars.[26] Some Princeton students had received A.E.S. aid during his own years as president. Nothing in his experience at Princeton, however, had prepared James Carnahan to comprehend the immense changes in the system of supporting indigent students that the A.E.S. outlined in 1826 and 1827.

Carnahan had been familiar with a kind of student assistance that was paternal and private; he still thought of aid as the responsibility of a student's own family, town, church, patron, or college. As the exchanges between Carnahan and Stuart progressed, eventually consuming 150 pages in the *Biblical Repertory* and the *American Quarterly Register*, the strangeness of the American Education Society impressed itself upon the public consciousness. Carnahan's critiques were like benchmarks, permitting a precise measurement of where, in its first fifteen years, the A.E.S. had passed beyond the conventional mind of Princeton, beyond traditional conceptions of charity. Stuart's rejoinders demonstrated the futility of measuring the A.E.S. in conventional terms.

The rhetoric of past debates may have a certain beauty in the present, the beauty of words forced from minds engaged in contest and challenge. Carnahan and Stuart stretched their minds. They were by necessity made conscious of what was old and what was new in their notions of students in relationship to their society. At the same time, the language of both men revealed that the American Education Society represented one manifestation of a social change that even they were only beginning to understand. Old ideas were passing from the consciousness of the nineteenth century, and the notions taking their place were utterly novel.

Loans and schedules contradicted every principle of charity known to Carnahan. He noted that A.E.S. loans were called "parental loans." "But parents do not usually take bonds of their children, to refund the money expended in their education," he said. Parents ought merely to expect gratitude from their children—besides the assurance of a secure old age in return for educating sons. Loans, on the other hand, appeared to cancel familial obligations. "If a father bind a son with legal bonds, he, at the same time, cancels that of filial duty." Schedules intruded upon the privacy of matters that once had been the proper concern only of an individual student and his family or patron. With all the suspicion of a man first encountering the documentary apparatus of a bureaucracy, Carnahan refused to believe that a kind of privacy might be found in the anonymity of a thousand schedules. The details required on this new form were "unnecessarily and painfully minute." Princeton students, he believed, could not bear to fill out schedules. "Young men of delicate and ingenuous feelings, shrink from this public developement of private and personal circumstances."[27]

Carnahan would have abolished the loans and schedules and revived a system of charity more suited to villages of a dozen houses. His attitude suggested that he wanted to support a smaller number of indigent students—these to be carefully chosen by individual churches and patrons from young men in the student population who already had been asked to enter the ministry. The men who selected beneficiaries would know beforehand the character and needs of the young men "whom we adopt," perhaps through having shared common experiences in the same town, church, or school. They would need no schedules. And aid would be entirely gratuitous, a true charity of the church. As he outlined his notions, Carnahan began to think of the Presbyterian church in familial terms. "She is their parent, their guardian," he said, "bound by the most sacred ties to give them spiritual nourishment and such an education as is suited to their capacity, and likely to be useful to the community of which they are members." As the "moral parent," the church should support her indigent sons while they studied, without demanding future repayment, without exacting promises to enter the ministry. In place of such legal bonds, Carnahan wanted to trust the personal bonds of gratitude of students toward their benefactors.[28]

Stuart was too defensive to rest his case upon the novelties implicit in Carnahan's application of family imagery to an institution as large as the Presbyterian church. Instead, he tried—without success—to apply the same stock of familial terms to the American Education Society. He professed to see nothing strange in parental loans and insisted that it was "no new thing" for parents to make loans to their children for education. He appealed to his own experience: he had several sons to educate but could not do so unless the older ones contributed to assist the younger ones. "I make this a condition of completing their education; and I have no scruples in doing so, although I would hope and trust that I am not deficient in parental tenderness." Other New England families, confronting the same problem of educating more than a single son, were adopting these arrangements. So was the A.E.S. Stuart denied that the schedule invaded domestic privacy. The information it gathered still remained private when held in confidence between the student, the head of his school ("who is or ought to be his most confidential and paternal friend"), and the directors of the A.E.S. ("who are also *in loco parentum*"). Moreover, the schedule served a parental function, helping instill "the virtues of industry, frugality, regularity of life, and caution as to unnecessary and injudicious expenses." In this sense, the schedule could be compared to a letter from a son at school, explaining how he had managed his affairs.[29]

Yet the analogy failed, as Stuart himself confessed. As his argument proceeded, he saw that A.E.S. loans were not really analogous to those made by a father to his son, since the funds were dispensed by the directors from the purses of donors scattered throughout the country, and required written security. "In these respects, therefore, it is far from being fair, to compare their situation with that of a parent." Stuart even came to realize the innovative character of the schedule, though without Carnahan's criticism he might never have done so. He knew that the schedule had not been adopted merely to enhance the character of beneficiaries or to teach them lessons of personal economy. The schedule justified its existence by the sheer value of the statistical information on student and college finances it permitted the society to gather; it provided, as Stuart acknowledged, "the basis of many of their calculations and their measures."[30] This formal document came into use because it was needed to process the requests of large numbers of indigent young men, scattered over unprecedented distances, confined to no single community or denomination, and sharing no common life with the directors who had decided to assist them. When an institution envisioned operations on a scale requiring a printed form like the A.E.S. schedule, it naturally ceased to function like a Presbyterian church, the Stuart family of Andover, or the College of New Jersey.

Simply by its immensity, the American Education Society transformed the situation confronting indigent students. No longer did these young men depend upon local institutions—churches, families, and schools—to make their decisions regarding education and careers. No longer did they find themselves under the control of these institutions or dependent upon them for support. No longer did they have to wait for a minister or a teacher to suggest their names for patronage, or for parents to pledge their support. They could offer themselves.

Once enrolled, the students governed decisions that shaped their daily lives, for the A.E.S. extended what it was in no position to deny: an unprecedented degree of independence—especially for charity students—and the status of self-reliant adults. Financial support came to them in regular, quarterly installments, and it followed them through their entire course of study. No longer did they have to ask for funds at the moment of need; no longer did their aid come exclusively in small, unpredictable sums that could be spared by a donor, or in the form of food, shoes, and cast-off pantaloons. The offering of loans, rather than gratuities, freed young men from the childish dependence of a charity student. Loans permitted young men to feel that they were not pensioners on charity but dependent upon themselves.[31] Strictly speaking, one could no longer speak of A.E.S. assistance as charity—or of the society as a charitable institution. With its system of loans, the A.E.S. became a vast mutual-aid society on a scale a thousand times greater than the Stuart or Hopkins families.

The texts of the exchanges between Carnahan and Stuart indicate an awareness on the part of both men that the A.E.S. was releasing indigent students from the restrictions and controls once imposed by local institutions. Yet their attention did not focus upon the implications of this change in terms of its impact upon student careers. Rather, their debate turned toward the more immediate consequences of the scale of A.E.S. operations, toward the power of this society over the student population and the ministerial profession.

Carnahan fixed most of his attention upon the vastness of the organization and upon the powers of its central office. "This Society is a national Society," he warned, "striving to become such in fact, as well as in name." It had branches in every section of the country; it sent agents into every state. No single denomination, college, or state controlled its funds or its students, whose loyalties, he predicted, would lie with the A.E.S., not with their individual churches, towns, or colleges. The society was organizing everywhere, even within the bounds of the Presbyterian church, "and bids fair, in a short time, to get the whole of this important business under its sole direction." As if prompted by premonitions of an ideological movement led by the A.E.S., he warned that its funds, together with its "zeal and constancy," might easily be employed in "the propagation of the most destructive opinions."[32]

In vain did Stuart protest that the society would not use its power to pull down any church or college, that it had sent its 900 students impartially to schools of every denomination and locale. This was exactly what Carnahan feared. The A.E.S. drew its membership and scattered its beneficiaries in a manner employed by no other institution. It had devised a scheme of organization so odd and potentially so influential that Carnahan called it a "foreign institution," unlike any he knew or could condone. Its leadership had gathered great power.

> And the organization is so adjusted, the machinery is so admirably arranged as to concentrate the whole power in a single point; so that the hand of an infant, touching a lever in Boston, can control, and manage, and direct the whole Christian community, south and west of the Connecticut, interested in this concern.[33]

The fear of this new lever, this new bureaucratic structure, can be attributed to Carnahan's wounded notions of proper Presbyterian polity. Sectarian jealousies and fears alone may have prompted his critique of the society; a man with these fears would have noted precisely the novelties that Carnahan detected in the A.E.S. Simply by the size of its disbursements, it could influence the curriculum in seminaries, colleges, and academies. Through its selection of beneficiaries, it could determine the social, religious, and ideological character of a significant portion of the student population, and ultimately of nearly all the ministry.

The debate between Carnahan and Stuart generated more than a consciousness that power was shifting from local institutions to a central agency in Boston; its significance lay not only in what it made clear about the society but also in the rationale it established for modifying the more alarming features of this new system of student aid. Though Carnahan's criticism did not lead to the dismantling of the A.E.S., circumstances gradually forced the directors to take his objections seriously.

Small deficiencies began to appear in A.E.S. budgets in the 1830s as the number of beneficiaries approached 1,000. After the panic of 1837, the society had to borrow money from Boston banks in order to maintain its beneficiary lists. Disappointment pursued the new schemes of fund raising, since poverty prevented most former beneficiaries from honoring their notes, and the directors canceled those of graduates who became missionaries or who settled in poor churches. Repayments yielded only a small fraction of the income needed by the society. After four years of struggle, it became clear that neither branches, agents, investments, refunds, nor borrowing could sustain an operation on the scale of the American Education Society. As late as October 1842, the directors insisted that they were not prepared "to propose any material modifications in the constitution of the Society," but they asked for the advice of those who favored changes.[34] Their invitation was accepted; the debate that James Carnahan began was renewed within the society itself, and this time Carnahan's opinions carried more weight.

The society began a general retrenchment in the scale of its operations after 1843. It ceased to accept applications from students in academies, effectively restricting recruitment to the colleges and theological seminaries. Between 1840 and 1845 it reduced the number of beneficiaries from 922 to 345, and it never again extended its lists to the level of the 1830s.[35] It began once again to offer grants, making the loan arrangement optional. Selection and supervision became more rigorous. In 1874 the A.E.S. was merged with the Society for the Promotion of Collegiate and Theological Education at the West, and it began to channel much of its aid to students through the colleges, though it continued to support its own beneficiaries until the early twentieth century. Although the society survived in muted institutional forms into the twentieth century, it ceased to dominate student charity. The A.E.S. did, however, stimulate the reinvention of the scholarship at American colleges, whose student-aid funds grew immensely after the Civil War. The bureaucratic organization at Boston, created in a period when local institutions of charity had become inadequate or had ceased to exist at all, never again held the power it gathered between 1815 and 1840.

Nevertheless, none of these modifications restored the system of intimate community patronage to the position it had occupied before the rise of the American Education Society. None of them shifted powers over student patronage back to institutions that functioned at the community level, as Carnahan had envisioned. Even the colleges he had known ceased, like Yale, to be local institutions after the Civil War. The changes of the early nineteenth century were not reversed. In its most influential period, between 1815 and 1840, the American Education Society irrevocably established the material conditions and administrative structure that expanded the options of indigent students, making it possible for them to be independent of local institutions in making important decisions in life. The first expansion of these options beyond what the villages could provide came through a bureaucracy—a bureaucracy created to encompass their own unprecedented numbers.

Notes

1 Cash Book, October 26, 1815, to April 1826, American Education Society Archives, Congregational Library, Boston, Mass. The society was incorporated as the American Society for Educating Pious Youth for the Gospel Ministry, but it changed its official name in 1819.

2 *Fiftieth Annual Report of the Directors of the American Education Society* (Boston: T. R. Marvin, 1866), p. 11; "View of the American Colleges, 1833," *American Quarterly Register* 5 (1833): 332-33.

3 *Fourth Report of the Directors of the American Society for Educating Pious Youth for the Gospel Ministry* (Andover, Mass.: Flagg and Gould, 1819), p. 17; *Ninth Annual Report of the Directors of the American Education Society* (Boston: Crocker & Brewster, 1824), pp. 5-6.

4 This analysis of the A.E.S. has been influenced strongly by Max Weber's theory of bureaucracy. See Hans Gerth and C. Wright Mills, eds. and trans., *From Max Weber: Essays in Sociology* (New York: Oxford University Press, 1946), pp. 196-244. I owe the language and statement in this paragraph to the brilliant work of Charles Bowden, "Ashfield Skyline: A Look at 19th Century Notions About Health" (Ph.D. diss., University of Wisconsin, 1972). See also Lynn Marshall, "The Strange Stillbirth of the Whig Party," *American Historical Review* 72 (1967): 445-68; Donald G. Mathews, "The Second Great Awakening as an Organizing Process, 1780-1830: An Hypothesis," *American Quarterly* 21 (1969): 23-43; Bertram Wyatt-Brown, *Lewis Tappan and the Evangelical War Against Slavery* (Cleveland: Press of Case Western Reserve University, 1969), pp. 226-47; and Leonard L. Richards, *"Gentlemen of Property and Standing": Anti-Abolition Mobs in Jacksonian America* (New York: Oxford University Press, 1970), pp. 47-49, 55-62, 74-81, 167-70. Cf. Stanley M. Elkins, *Slavery: A Problem in American Institutional and Intellectual Life* (Chicago: University of Chicago Press, 1959), pp. 140-222.

5 "Letter," *American Quarterly Register* 7 (1835): 371-76.

6 *Twelfth Annual Report of the Directors of the American Education Society* (Andover, Mass.: Flagg and Gould, 1828), p. 4; Bela Bates Edwards, *Writings of Professor B. B. Edwards, with a Memoir by Edwards A. Park*, 2 vols. (Boston: John P. Jewett & Co., 1853), 1:71-72.

7 Minutes of examination of applicants, July 9, 1816, July 9, 1817, and October 8, 1817, Box 6, Park Family Papers, Yale University Library, New Haven, Conn. For letters from agents stressing the importance of revivals between 1830 and 1836, see *American Quarterly Register*, vols. 3-9, passim.

8 Cushman to William Cogswell, September 15, 1831, Beneficiary Letters, A.E.S. Archives; *Seventeenth Annual Report of the Directors of the American Education Society* (Boston: Perkins & Marvin, 1833), p. 77.

9 "Board of Education of the General Assembly," *American Quarterly Register* 6 (1833): 136; "Board of Education of the General Assembly of the Presbyterian Church," *American Quarterly Register* 13 (1840): 119-21; R. C. Mills, "History of the Northern Baptist Education Society," *One Hundred and Second Anniversary of the Northern Baptist Education Society* (Boston: C. H. Simonds & Co., 1893), p. 135; *An Historical Sketch of the Board of Education and of the Permanent Committee on Education of the Presbyterian Church in the United States of America, 1819-1888* (Philadelphia: Board of Education, 1889), pp. 7-8. See also Jesse B. Sears, *Philanthropy in the History of American Higher Education* (Washington, D.C.: Government Printing Office, 1922), pp. 47-51, 73-78.

10 *Fourth Report of the A.E.S.*, pp. 12-15.

11 *Seventh Report of the Directors of the American Education Society* (Andover, Mass.: Flagg and Gould, 1822), p. 4; *Tenth Annual Report of the Directors of the American Education Society* (Andover, Mass.: Flagg and Gould, 1826), p. 7.

12 Bela Bates Edwards, *Memoir of the Rev. Elias Cornelius* (Boston: Perkins & Marvin, 1833), pp. 206-76; idem, *Writings of Edwards*, 1:72; *Twelfth Report of the A.E.S.*, p. 12.

13 See the rules printed in the annual reports of the society.

14 "Memo of business etc. of the Directors of Amer. Soc. for Educating etc.," July 10, 1816, Box 6, Park Family Papers, Yale University Library, New Haven, Conn.

15 *Seventh Report of the A.E.S.*, pp. 17-18.

16 *Eleventh Annual Report of the Directors of the American Education Society* (Andover, Mass.: Flagg and Gould, 1827), p. 23; *Twelfth Report of the A.E.S.*, p. 11; *Seventeenth Report of the A.E.S.*, p. 40; Edwards, *Writings of Edwards*, 1:70; *Nineteenth Annual Report of the Directors of the American Education Society* (Boston: T. R. Marvin & Son, 1835), pp. 42-43.

17 Cornelius to the young men under the patronage of the A.E.S. in Hamilton College, July 14, 1827, Letter Book 1, A.E.S. Archives; William Cogswell, *Letters to*

Young Men Preparing for the Christian Ministry (Boston: Perkins & Marvin, 1837).

18 *Seventh Report of the A.E.S.*, p. 23.

19 *Fifteenth Annual Report of the Directors of the American Education Society* (Boston: Perkins & Marvin, 1831), p. 21; Cogswell to Ansel Clark, February 16, 1835, Letter Book 2, A.E.S. Archives.

20 Cogswell to John Spaulding, December 6, 1836; Cogswell to Benjamin Tappan, March 2, 1837; Cogswell to William Allen, February 28, 1837, all in Letter Book 2, A.E.S. Archives; Samuel Riddel to T. D. Kimball, n.d.; Riddel to Abrahm Peters et al., March 28, 1850, Letter Book 3, A.E.S. Archives.

21 Constitution and subscribers' names, August 29, 1815, art. 4, A.E.S. Archives; *Eleventh Report of the A.E.S.*, p. 24; *Fifteenth Report of the A.E.S.*, pp. 16-17; *Seventeenth Report of the A.E.S.*, pp. 43-44.

22 *Sixth Report of the Directors of the American Education Society* (Andover, Mass.: Flagg and Gould, 1821), p. 4; *Sixteenth Annual Report of the Directors of the American Education Society* (Boston: Perkins & Marvin, 1832), p. 10.

23 *Sixth Report of the A.E.S.*, p. 4; *Eleventh Report of the A.E.S.*, pp. 21-22; Cogswell to William Patten, February 23, 1836, Letter Book 2, A.E.S. Archives.

24 Another study has seen American benevolent societies as applying to their own structures the models of English societies and consciously pursuing repressive aims. See Charles I. Foster, *An Errand of Mercy: The Evangelical United Front, 1790-1837* (Chapel Hill: University of North Carolina Press, 1960). Clifford S. Griffin also stresses their repressive nature in *Their Brothers' Keepers: Moral Stewardship in the United States, 1800-1865* (New Brunswick, N.J.: Rutgers University Press, 1960). Both of these studies differ from the interpretation here and in Mathews, "The Second Great Awakening," pp. 23-43.

25 [James Carnahan], "The General Assembly's Board of Education and the American Education Society," *Biblical Repertory*, n.s., 1 (1829): 369. The article was unsigned but was attributed to Carnahan by the editors in a subsequent issue, as was the second article in the series; I have attributed to Carnahan all three articles on the A.E.S. that appeared under the name of the editors of the *Biblical Repertory*. See [James Carnahan], "Professor Stuart's Postscript to His Letter to the Editors of the Biblical Repertory," *Biblical Repertory*, n.s., 2 (1830): 125.

26 John Maclean, *History of the College of New Jersey*, 2 vols. (Philadelphia: J. B. Lippincott & Co., 1877), 2:262-98.

27 [Carnahan], "Board of Education," pp. 356-58; idem, "Remarks of the Editors on the Foregoing Strictures," *Biblical Repertory*, n.s., 1 (1829): 611.

28 [Carnahan], "Board of Education," p. 357; idem, "Professor Stuart's Postscript," pp. 130-31; idem, "Remarks of the Editors," p. 607.

29 Moses Stuart, "Examination of the Review of the American Education Society," *Biblical Repertory*, n.s., 1 (1829): 567-76.

30 Ibid., pp. 565-76. Most of these schedules appear to have been lost; a few survive in the A.E.S. Archives.

31 *Eleventh Report of the A.E.S.*, pp. 20-21; *Sixteenth Report of the A.E.S.*, p. 19.

32 [Carnahan], "Remarks of the Editors," pp. 602-03, 616, 620, 622-23.

33 [Carnahan], "Board of Education," pp. 363-64.

34 Samuel Riddel to Samuel T. Armstrong, September 24, 1841, Letter Book 3, A.E.S. Archives; "Statement Submitted to the American Education Society," *American Quarterly Register* 15 (1842): 210-11, 218.

35 *Fiftieth Report of the A.E.S.*, pp. 11-12. For a comprehensive study of the A.E.S., see Natalie Ann Naylor, "Raising a Learned Ministry: The American Education Society, 1815-1860" (Ph.D. diss., Columbia University, 1971).

PART III

Poverty's Toll
on Student Life

Penniless scholars affected the style and tone of student life. They imposed their need for economy upon college arrangements for food and shelter. Certain amenities had to be abandoned altogether for several generations because of this tyrannous poverty, this material necessity. Young gentlemen who sought refinement did so on their own. After a period of intermingling, the social classes separated at New England colleges. Amenities did return in the second half of the century, but in the meantime the colleges had changed.

In seeking their own social survival and advancement, the poor and indigent took charge of their own lives. They found their own money, work, board, and room, and they did not depend on the college treasury. Now they introduced, not only frugality, but also a new independence to student life, an independence that was shared by all students, rich and poor. In so doing, they undermined collegiate authority. Eventually, the influx of the poor, together with changes in the material conditions of daily student life, altered the intellectual experience as well.

6 Self-Reliance: The Demise of Community

Those who wished to be educated at Yale . . . were compelled to accept this indiscriminate intermingling of the rich and the poor. Yale College in 1822 was the most democratic portion of American society.

Julian Sturtevant (Yale, 1826)

By the time Ira Young earned his bachelor's degree from Dartmouth College in 1828, he was twenty-seven years old. His father, a carpenter in Lebanon, New Hampshire, had not financed his son's education. After Ira turned sixteen, he taught every winter in the district schools of the neighborhood, and until he came of age he worked in his father's trade. At maturity, he determined to prepare for college. For eight months he worked with his hands—perhaps as a carpenter—and earned enough money for one year's study at Meriden Academy, after which he entered Dartmouth. "Neither in this year of preparation, nor all his college course, did he ever receive pecuniary aid from any individual or society," declared his biographer. "He paid his way by teaching."[1] His poverty dictated a budget in which income was derived from self-help, and expenditure was controlled by strict economy. Hence, his teaching and his choice of Dartmouth, six miles from home. For every item of his accounts, he relied upon himself.

Student life as it had to be lived by poor young men like Ira Young demanded its own peculiar style. In the presence of a student population of mixed social origins which contained many men like Young, a residential collegiate community became an impossibility, although this form of college had evolved in colonial New England as the traditional ideal. Students once had been expected to gather permanently inside the college and reside there, withdrawing from adult society for all but a few weeks of vacation each year. The poor, who could afford only the essentials in student life, made this gathering in seclusion impossible. They needed very cheap board and room, cheaper than some more affluent students would tolerate. Their budgets did not permit them to withdraw from the economy of adult society for whole years: they needed time to work. Between 1800 and 1840, therefore, the old collegiate community disappeared in New England, changing the style of student life entirely. Students went into towns and countryside for food and lodging and work, mixing promiscuously with the adult society, relying upon themselves.

Reasons of economy had compelled Ira Young to stay near home for his education, though he could not have commuted even six miles each day without a reliable horse. Students who could return to their parents' homes each day for food and lodging never comprised a very large part of the college enrollment. At Williams College in 1822, only eight of forty-nine students came from Williamstown families; at Amherst in 1822, only nine of ninety-eight came from the town of Amherst.[2] The major saving came to those who lived too far to commute but close enough to spare themselves long journeys between home and campus, a significant consideration before the railroad era.

The difficulty and expense of travel—especially before the railroad—might have discouraged anyone from going far for education. Poor students traveled in the manner of the lower classes, walking and begging rides. When Emory Washburn set out for Williams College in 1815, he owned no horse, so he relied on "stage and chance." From his home in Leicester, in central Massachusetts, he took the stage west to Pittsfield, "and thence by a providential team or carriage the remainder of my journey."

> I have often smiled as I have recalled with what persevering assiduity I waylaid every man who passed by the hotel, in order to find some one who would consent to take as a passenger a luckless wight in pursuit of an education under such difficulties.[3]

In 1822 Julian Sturtevant and his companions traveled 500 miles, from Ohio to New Haven, with an old wagon and their minister's retired horse.

> Our mode of traveling was not new, and it already had the name of "ride and tie." Our wagon could only furnish seats for two, and our horse must not be overtaxed. Two of us drove three or four miles, tied the horse by the road side, and walked on. The others walked till they came to the horse and in their turn rode three or four miles, passing the first two on the way.[4]

While a majority of students came from nearby areas and avoided long journeys like Sturtevant's, most of them still had to make arrangements for food and shelter beyond the parental roof. Especially at the provincial colleges, where the poor concentrated, these arrangements began to depart radically from communal tradition.

Until the nineteenth century, colleges expected students to dine together in commons and share living quarters within college buildings, under college supervision. Harvard devised its laws of 1655 with this expectation in mind: "Noe Student shall board or lye out of the Colledge without just Cause allowed by the President."[5] No colonial college ever did gather all students at its own tables or within its own rooms. Many exceptions occurred, like those in 1725 at Harvard, when compensation had to be paid to the butler or steward because significant numbers of students were dining out of commons. Colonial students, moreover, retained a kind of medieval casualness about routines and calendars, particularly in an age when travel entailed unpredictable delays. Often they returned late, drifting slowly back to school despite warnings against such tardiness. These lapses were unpredictable, however, and had nothing to do with the students' economic disabilities. Most students through 1750 did dine in commons and live in college halls. Whenever conditions became too lax, students would find themselves being admonished for lateness and forced again into college quarters. The assumption prevailed that the kind of secluded living arrangements of colleges in Elizabethan England were normal and that departures from this standard were exceptional and temporary.[6]

In the second half of the eighteenth century, the residential system at Harvard and Yale began to erode. As the student population grew, both institutions began to enroll students more varied in their social origins; that is, they began admitting larger numbers of the poor. This change revealed itself in the growing presence of mature young men. At Harvard, the portion of students enrolling after their twenty-first birthdays and graduating after their twenty-fifth rose from 8.5 percent in 1761-70, to 13.3 percent in 1771-80, 17.4 percent in 1781-90, and 18.7 percent in 1791-1800. Yale experienced the same phenomenon, although more briefly and in slightly lesser degrees. By the decade ending in 1800, nearly a fifth of Harvard's students were entering as adults.[7] In providing for students from different social classes, college officials found it difficult to maintain even their ideological commitment to the residential college.

After the middle of the eighteenth century, institutional erosion began to manifest itself in subtle ways. Harvard took account of the need for different routines and began to experiment with its ancient calendar. Both Harvard and Yale had trouble maintaining the college commons. Yale encountered difficulty even after President Clap had tried to force common dining and living upon Yale students at mid-eighteenth century. President Ezra Stiles, in his diary entry for November 1, 1779, listed seventy of eighty-eight students dining in commons. The catalog that Stiles compiled in 1780 showed seventy-seven students living in college, thirty-three in town, and eighteen in quarters unknown.[8] In the nineteenth century, the process of erosion would advance to ruin.

College officials tried for more than a century to maintain commons in the traditional form. The Harvard laws of 1734 prescribed such a commons in meticulous detail. They required professors, tutors, graduates, and virtually all undergraduates to dine in commons, excepting only the waiters and "such whose Parents or Guardians live so nigh that they may Conveniently board them," together with those excused in cases of necessity. At the tolling of the college bell, waiters were to "receive the Plates and Victualls at the

Kitchen Hatch, & carry the same to the severall tables for which they are designed." And tables were to be covered "with clean linnen cloaths, of a Suitable length & breadth twice a week." A steward supervised all arrangements.[9]

Communal dining in this style involved much more than convenience and economy. Commons was an instrument of discipline, manners, and power. The Harvard laws of 1734 required students to sit in their places, "behave themselves decently and orderly," and wait for the blessing before eating,

> and whosoever shall be rude or Clamourous at such time, or shall go out of the Hall before thanks be returned, Shall be punished by one of the Tutors, not exceeding five shillings.

Commons permitted the college to supervise students outside the classroom, as if they were schoolboys to be sheltered from temptations of the world. Commons made it unnecessary to frequent any "Tavern or Victualling House in Cambridge."[10]

Traditional commons survived until the mid-1820s at Harvard and Yale, thanks to a system of penalties and fines that made all other arrangements illegal or difficult.[11] Julian Sturtevant found commons still flourishing when he entered Yale in 1822 (though professors no longer attended). It served about 300 students, with seniors and sophomores crowded into the south room, juniors and freshmen into the north, and tutors seated on platforms overlooking all. Old formalities survived: one tutor struck the table "two or three smart blows" with the handle of his knife, commanding all to rise for the blessing. And this commons was still drawing all social types together. "That group of students was a strange medly," Sturtevant said. In the same room dined sons of wealthy eastern merchants, poor New England farmers, aristocratic planters, and Ohio backwoodsmen; "and even the humblest sons of daily toil were there, sitting at the same tables."

> However distasteful this might be to many, there was no help for it. Those who wished to be educated at Yale . . . were compelled to accept this indiscriminate intermingling of the rich and the poor. Yale College in 1822 was the most democratic portion of American society.[12]

That was 1822. By 1827 no one at Yale was compelled to accept this intermingling, for the college had begun to board poor students in ways that segregated them from the rich and divided the student body according to social and economic class. By 1860 the old assumption that all students should dine together—which had persisted despite contradictions in practice—disappeared, and alternative arrangements ceased to be looked upon as exceptions to the rule.

It was the poor, primarily, who brought down the commons. Commons declined because it could not incorporate large numbers of students like Julian Sturtevant, who wanted their fare either cheaper than the steward could provide at a profit or simpler than more affluent students would tolerate. This dilemma became critical in the early nineteenth century. Commons could not be maintained for the affluent without excluding the poor, who, having no scholarships, had to rely on the cheapness of food. Late in the eighteenth century, Harvard ordered the steward to keep the charge for commons "as low as possible" and prescribed ways to make the diet more ascetic for all scholars, who were required to dine together. This attempt to keep costs within the range of poor students dissatisfied others and involved the students, the steward, and the college in unending feuds over food.[13] Disputes over commons came to represent more than frivolous complaints. They became economic wrangles between social classes over the style of student life, and they disrupted the old dining arrangements.

In theory, there were several ways to resolve the dilemma. At Harvard in the seventeenth century, the rich and the poor sat together, and extra dishes may have been provided for the rich to share with the poor.[14] This arrangement appears not to have been considered anywhere in the early nineteenth century and would have seemed repugnant had it been rediscovered. In 1758 the Harvard Overseers proposed to permit students to form themselves into messes no larger than eight in number and arrange with the steward for their diet. The Harvard Corporation (and probably the steward, too) rejected the proposal as too complicated and expensive; it would have made commons into a restaurant.[15] At some Scottish universities, where large numbers of poor students enrolled, it was customary to have two tables in commons, one less expensive than the other. In effect, this meant providing two commons, one for the poor and one for the affluent.[16]

Yale College actually tried a variation of this last plan beginning in the mid-1820s, shortly after Julian Sturtevant enrolled. The need for inexpensive food had become so pressing by this time that Yale initiated a "cheap boarding house" operated by the steward especially for the poor, where they could obtain food "at a lower rate than it is furnished in commons."[17] In 1830 board at the cheap hall was one dollar and twenty-five cents per week, compared to one dollar and sixty cents at the regular commons.

Harvard abandoned compulsory commons in 1825 and for a number of years thereafter considered its dining hall an institution for the poor, or "those whose circumstances or inclinations may render it preferable." Other students were finally released to find better fare in the town. Simultaneously, Harvard tried to continue levying a ten-dollar fee on all students—whether they dined in the hall or not—as a subsidy for those who, "from economy or other motives, board in Commons."[18]

This experiment and the one at Yale effectively destroyed the old idea of commons, for students from different social classes were either segregated or released from the regular commons according to their ability to pay. Neither experiment survived long. Yale abandoned its cheap boardinghouse in 1839, and the last mention of any commons at the college came in the catalog of 1844-45.[19] Harvard renounced all efforts to provide board in 1849.[20] Even so, the commons—though it functioned only for the poor—had survived much longer at Harvard and Yale than at the provincial colleges. Bowdoin, Brown, and Dartmouth had abandoned it by 1815. Williams, Vermont, Middlebury, and Amherst were founded without commons and established none before the Civil War. In their place, there developed around these campuses a variety of less formal arrangements that permitted students to find board in as sparing, or as lavish, a style as possible.

At Williams College, a traveler in 1796 found students boarding at two large taverns in Williamstown, a practice forbidden at older colleges until far into the nineteenth century.[21] Mark Hopkins boarded at the hotel kept by Mr. Hawkes when he enrolled at Williams in 1822. "He has 16 boarders," he wrote his brother Harry; "board is 8 shillings."[22] The Williams catalog advertised the price of local board at a dollar to a dollar and thirty-four cents a week; "Good board may be had for a dollar by walking a mile."[23] Albert Hopkins, who was running into debt at Williams, ate at some kind of a boardinghouse in 1823-24, his first year in college. "I board at Noyens, and like boarding there very well," he wrote to Harry Hopkins; "he has ten, or twelve boarders." Albert also found it "very fashionable" for students to board themselves in the college buildings, preparing their own food. "Some fellows boarded themselves last term for ten cents a week."[24]

Self-boarding appeared everywhere, often with the encouragement of the colleges, which permitted students to keep food in their rooms. Its appeal lay in economy. Student account books indicate that some students were spending as little as $100 for forty weeks of schooling at Williams and Amherst in the early 1820s; at a dollar or two per week, expenditures for food might account for nearly half the year's expenses. Almost in the manner of the middle ages, poor scholars in the early nineteenth century foraged for themselves, sometimes just to supplement the board they obtained at local inns or with families. Charles U. Shepard (Amherst, 1825) witnessed food-gathering expeditions of poor students at Amherst in its earliest years.

> The orchards were far better than now; the finest of peaches grew in abundance. The College grounds gave us all the chestnuts we wanted, and the hickory groves furnished boundless supplies of walnuts. If we craved other drink than that afforded by the unrivaled College well, we could go to the cider mills and fill our buckets. In the winter, too, there was shooting or other hunting, witness the hound of one of our early students. . . .[25]

Between 1800 and 1840 it became customary for students to board with families in town or on nearby farms; no longer was this considered exceptional, and by 1850 it did not require special permission at most colleges. Boarding with families became the most expensive way to dine in these years, but the range of choice was wide, and an occasional family would board a student for the sake of charity.[26] Family dining was actually an old arrangement; it had existed periodically in colonial college towns and survives today in rare instances. As the number of students boarding with families increased in the early nineteenth century, however, new institutions began to evolve from the family dining room, offering a greater variety of fare than commons ever served.

By 1840 some family dining rooms, having accepted as many as ten or more boarders, assumed the character of boardinghouses, and they began to be called by that term in college catalogs of the 1830s and 1840s.[27] Women frequently ran these establishments as family operations, using other members of the family to help them. Soon, the boardinghouse became a full-time job, and students gathered at all-student tables instead of mixing with the family. William Hammond (Amherst, 1849) boarded at one such establishment at Amherst in 1846. Hammond, who was fifteen, had to arrange for his own meals, since the college provided no commons. He was accepted as a boarder by an elderly Mrs. Ferry, who, with the assistance of her daughter, served three meals a day for eight or nine other students. In fact, Hammond discovered, the other boarders had determined his acceptance, for by this time a select student society was patronizing Mrs. Ferry's establishment.[28] Identical developments in other boardinghouses eventually transformed many of them into a new sort of institution, the separate *fraternity house* built by students themselves, in which they both dined and lived with a select society, never mingling with the poor.

For poor students, another kind of institution began to appear alongside the boardinghouse. This was the boarding club, association, or company, actually run by students. Among the earliest of these was the association formed at Bowdoin College in 1824 to provide cheaper board than families offered. Its members purchased a dozen cows, preserved meat, did their own marketing, and worked cooperatively in the dining hall, cutting the extra costs of the old commons system, with its steward, waiters, and tablecloths of linen. The Bowdoin Visiting Committee noted every virtue and novelty of this establishment in 1829.

> The students provide commons for themselves of a good quality at a very economical rate, the expense not exceeding $1.16 a week. The entire police of the establishment is under the students themselves and we are happy in being able to say that every degree of order and decorum is observed that can be desired furnishing a very convincing proof of the capability of the students to govern themselves when they are under no other restraints than their own personal convenience and sense of propriety.[29]

Except for boarding alone in dormitory rooms, student clubs provided the least expensive food. When the Yale catalog first recognized their existence in 1839, the clubs were offering cheaper board than the college commons and had replaced the college-owned "cheap boarding hall." In 1841 they were less expensive by far than New Haven's boardinghouses; at Amherst by 1842 they were cheaper than dining with families.[30]

Clubs like these did not evolve from earlier institutions, though in some cases they assumed the characteristics of the old commons or boardinghouse. The association at Bowdoin did occupy a college-owned building and it did gather most of the students, but it was founded ten years after the demise of the old Bowdoin commons. These clubs were entirely new institutions, performing a function that the collegiate community itself could no longer encompass.

Colleges had greater success in sheltering students, though here, too, they rarely found it possible to gather all their students within their walls. They could never build enough dormitories—or "colleges"—to match increasing enrollments; there were always periods when many students found rooms in town. This became increasingly true during the course of the nineteenth century.

Yale introduced special housing for indigents in the 1820s, when it began to permit the poor to occupy recitation rooms at night, offering them a chance to "save their room rent and fuel in winter, and receive a small compensation in summer."[31] In 1851 this option was restricted to impoverished freshmen; in 1859 the custom disappeared entirely at Yale, without having spread to other colleges.

Elsewhere, residence buildings constructed by the colleges served the needs of the poor, a function their very appearance still betrays: plain, almost primitive structures were built in the early nineteenth century, with no luxuries. Emory Washburn lived in East College at Williams between 1815 and 1818.

> Not one of the rooms or passage-ways was painted. [Not] one of the rooms was papered, or ever had a carpet upon it. And I do not believe the entire furniture of any one room, excepting perhaps the bed, could have cost, or would have sold for, five dollars.[32]

North College at Amherst, occupied for the first time in 1822-23, followed the same plan; no room had a carpet, only one room had blinds, and not half a dozen were painted, according to one contemporary description. "We all made our own fires and took the entire care of our rooms," recalled Alonzo Chapin, who lived in North College that first year; "most of us sawed our own wood."[33]

Until late in the century, rooms in college always came unfurnished, so students could barter and buy their own chairs, desks, beds, and bedding, cheaply if they had to. The old custom of providing such services as sweeping and bedmaking disappeared everywhere, and most students now gathered their own wood. By renting only the bare room and making everything else optional, colleges kept rents within the range of the poorest students—even offering rooms free at times. College rooms at Williams rented at about nine dollars a year, with only slight variations, between the 1820s and 1872, when the minimum went up to fifteen dollars. Yale and Amherst charged about the same amount through the 1850s; rents were slightly higher at Harvard—more services were provided—and lower at other, provincial colleges. No institution offered a wide range of accommodations; rooms were uniformly austere.[34]

In the 1850s a demand for better accommodations within the colleges began to grow. The affluent classes would tolerate barracks no longer. Charles Bristed, who wrote an account of his five years at Cambridge University and compared English college life with what he had experienced at Yale, called for more services, especially in cleaning rooms. The Yale catalog for 1855 began to list a modest range of accommodations, renting for $7.50 to $16.50 a year; and in 1856 it suggested for the first time that room rent included a certain amount of "care." In 1858 Amherst opened a luxury dormitory containing a large portion of single rooms. By 1889 rents in Harvard dormitories ranged from \$25.00 to \$350.00. Yale students could pay from \$1.00 to \$24.00 a month for rent and could hire, for \$25.00 a year, a "private servant, for special care of room."[35]

Before 1860, however, the housing of the poor received more attention than the comfort of the rich, if only because the colleges themselves found luxury beyond their means. And since enrollment generally exceeded capacity, it became difficult to prevent large numbers of students from scattering among the population of the adult community. In the towns, there were rooms for a class who could afford rents two or three times higher than those in college, and cheap rooms might be found with charitable families or in dilapidated quarters.[36] The percentage of students living in town rooms before the Civil War varied throughout the region, and it fluctuated over time at individual institutions, reflecting differences in local housing conditions and changes in enrollments. Still, a shift did occur in the pattern of student housing between 1820 and 1860, with more and more students living in the towns.

At Yale in the 1820s, about 25 percent lived in town rooms; in the 1850s, more than 58 percent did so, an average of 266 students a year rooming in the city of New Haven, excluding those in the medical, law, theological and philosophical departments. At Dartmouth in the 1850s, those taking rooms in town exceeded 59 percent of the student body, or an average of 115 undergraduates per year residing in the private dwellings of Hanover. At other institutions, both urban and rural, the trend was almost as pronounced, generally reaching a peak of 30 to 40 percent between the 1830s and the 1850s.[37]

Initially, crowding within the colleges caused most of the movement into town. Financially pressed colleges simply could not build enough residence halls to house their increasing numbers of students. Despite the general trend, however, students continued to prefer cheaper rooms in college. Typically, most freshmen began by taking town rooms, and then drifted slowly into the college as they approached their senior years. Each class gradually moved into residence halls as it advanced through its four-year course, achieving seniority and first claim to college rooms. By midcentury, though, some wealthier students were preferring to remain in more expensive town rooms rather than take quarters in aging college buildings. Larger portions of senior classes remained in town, and the colleges did not always house so many students as their capacities had once permitted. An elevation in taste, then, began to act as another cause of shifting student residence, along with crowding and decay of buildings.

After 1860 the trend toward town reversed itself; colleges collected money to construct new residence halls, and some students gathered in fraternity houses. Thus larger numbers of students could be housed according to individual tastes within college-affiliated buildings. In the first half of the century, however, a strong secular trend toward town produced a scattered residential pattern among students. Perhaps President Stiles had observed an early development of this pattern when he made his catalog of 1780. Certainly crowding was no new phenomenon; the difference was that, between 1800 and 1860, scattering became a constant pattern in student housing, involving far greater numbers of students. College officials had ceased to expect students to live in any other pattern. Scattering gained acceptance and became an ordinary custom of student life. It also dispersed the collegiate community.

Indigent students tended to gather in older dormitory buildings as the century wore on, inheriting rooms that the affluent had abandoned in favor of better places in town or in new residence halls and fraternity houses. Almost without exception, beneficiaries of the American Education Society at Amherst College lived in dormitories before the Civil War, a period when as many as half the Amherst students favored rooms in the village at certain times.[38] Southern students at Yale, among the wealthiest in New Haven, gradually moved out of the colleges and into private rooms in town between 1820 and 1860. In 1827, fifty-six Southerners lived in college, fifteen in town; in 1850, only seven took rooms in college, forty-six in town.[39] In housing, therefore, as in dining arrangements, the rich and the poor were becoming separated, and the power to control these matters was shifting into new hands.

As the student population dispersed through the towns, taking rooms with families, in rooming houses, in hotels and inns, and finally in houses maintained by students themselves, new options and liberties opened for students of all social classes. Self-reliance and self-determination replaced the common experience of life in the old college community. Even those who remained in college rooms now did so by choice; and there they found themselves in command of their own lives, for the officials who once had lived in or near these buildings had scattered, too, leaving the occupants to supervise themselves with only the assistance of a tutor their own age.

It was the need to encompass both the poor and the upper classes that caused this fragmentation and collapse of the residential college, the crucial institution of the old collegiate community. With the infiltration by the poor, college officials of the early nineteenth century had to abandon the assumption that students must be fed and housed in a secluded, self-contained community. They found it impossible to accommodate the range of taste and need that accompanied the mixture of social classes within such small institutions.

It was the poor who finally shattered the old conception of proper routine in the collegiate community with their need for work—more work than anyone could find within the college. The poor, with their maddening absences for weeks on end, disrupted the progress of all students through the curriculum. They disrupted the old collegiate calendar and the cycle of long school terms broken only by brief vacations. Just as their need for economy spatially dispersed the collegiate community, their self-reliance and need for work dispersed that community through time. The periods when everyone gathered together became shorter and fewer.

Certainly no one thought it a new spectacle to see students like Ira Young at Dartmouth working their way through college, for collegiate life had always permitted a few poor students to earn their keep within the college. In the years between the Revolution and the Civil War, however, the kinds of work that students were finding began to change. With this change came a new conception of the place of labor in a student's life, a conception that differed profoundly from older notions.

In the colonial period, students earned their way by performing within the college the tasks of domestic servants and boys.[40] Wherever the college or its steward operated a commons, some poor students could work as waiters, serving their teachers and fellow students. Until the 1840s, waiters at Yale were allowed their board, supplemented by food that other students did not eat; usually they did not dine in commons themselves, since they worked while others ate.[41] Other jobs within the college required the poor to serve as faculty agents or assistants in petty recordkeeping. Most colleges appointed monitors who kept a record of absences, tardiness, and fines or penalties. Colonial Harvard and Yale also appointed scholars of the house, who kept accounts of damages to buildings, furnishings, and grounds. A few students worked as amanuenses, copying manuscripts and books almost in the manner of the modern graduate assistant or secretary. Remuneration for these tasks was small and probably did not provide complete support for any poor scholar.[42]

The virtue of this system of college labor was the ease with which its tasks could be incorporated into the students' daily lives and managed by officials of the institution. Waiters earned their board during the meal hours; monitors, scholars of the house, and copiers could work in spare time. The skills involved were simple ones acquired in the dining room or study. Moreover, the faculty could determine the appointment, tenure, and compensation of each student, who neither left the college to perform his tasks nor negotiated with employers outside the institution. His income and supervision were controlled entirely by the college. Under these conditions the college community might remain intact.

Until the late decades of the eighteenth century, the rhythm of college routines discouraged forms of work that might take the student away from his books, even for a portion of the day. Recitation and routine exercises absorbed most of his time; students at Yale in 1726 had free periods only at mealtime and between evening prayers and nine o'clock, which made daily work outside the college an unlikely option for most undergraduates.[43] Moreover, the long summer vacation as it now exists did not develop until after the Civil War. Harvard and Yale originally expected to keep school in session throughout the year, with only brief vacations. By 1745 Yale was allowing a six-week recess after fall commencement and a two-week recess in May. Those who tarried longer were subject to fines.[44] Students could not have earned a significant portion of their funds away from the college in these brief periods. Consequently, to avoid leaving school and displeasing the faculty, they had to find much of their work within the institution.

These kinds of work diminished in the early nineteenth century. Waiterships disappeared with the commons; some students continued to wait on tables, but they did so either in clubs or in private establishments outside the college. The position of monitor survived in most New England colleges throughout the nineteenth century, despite a growing hesitation by students to serve as agents of discipline; but here, too, there were changes. Monitorships were combined with the beneficiary fund at Harvard in the mid-1820s, when President Kirkland ordered a retrenchment in college expenditures. The college ceased to pay the salaries of monitors and required charity students to assume their duties. Kirkland's retrenchment also called for dismissing the president's secretary, who had assumed the functions of the student copiers—and would assume those functions again when the financial crisis had passed.[45] By the latter half of the nineteenth century, most colleges had created the beginnings of a professional secretarial staff, along with positions for custodians and janitors who performed the duties of the old scholar of the house.

The situation in which college officials could look upon working students as domestic servants ended in the early nineteenth century and did not revive before 1870, when universities began to require some of these old forms of work. In the meantime, colleges had to sanction forms of work that conflicted with a student's life, that threatened to change long-established, unconscious notions about his proper activities and the course of his schooling. They were forced to make new provisions in their calendars and daily routines to accommodate students with needs, like Ira Young's, for a season to keep school and a period to work with their hands. As students increasingly found work as schoolkeepers or manual laborers, they found themselves drawn away from their books into the economic life of the surrounding society. Dependence upon the collegiate community gave way to self-reliance; with this change students achieved a new autonomy.

Account books and budgets surviving from the first half of the nineteenth century suggest that students were able to rely on themselves almost entirely in making their way through college. Theophilus Packard (Amherst, 1823) spent a total of $406.63 for four years of college at Williams and Amherst, a figure that probably represented a minimum expenditure for a parsimonious young man; Packard noted every penny he spent.[46] Daniel Bliss (Amherst, 1854) demonstrated that it was still possible to spend only $126.81 for a year at Amherst a generation later, though Bliss became more extravagant during his next three years and wound up paying $975.44 for his whole course, with each expenditure carefully itemized in his book. What is striking about the accounts of Daniel Bliss are his sources of income: he was totally independent of both his family and his college for support. In four years Bliss took in $1,033.80. From his family he received a total of $13.00. From the college trustees he borrowed $28.00, together with additional notes of almost $300.00 for tuition; he deferred payment on these notes until after graduation. From the American Education Society he was granted $220.00, which he did not have to repay. Through his own efforts he earned the rest—$439.08. Almost half of his income came through work. This included slightly more than $250.00 for manual labor and $185.75 for eleven weeks of teaching in 1852, during his sophomore year. Had he taught every winter he might have earned everything for himself, though this would have taken him away from Amherst for three additional winters.[47]

Keeping school had not appeared suddenly as a new practice in the nineteenth century. Prior to 1800, recent graduates of Harvard and Yale often taught before entering their professions, and colonial students still in the midst of their college courses often took short-term jobs as teachers. Josiah Cotton (Harvard, 1698) left school in the winter of his sophomore year to teach the town school in his father's parsonage at Plymouth.[48] Gradually, larger numbers of undergraduates took up schoolkeeping as a way to finance their education. In the first half of the nineteenth century, at least one-third of all New England students took leaves of absence each year after the winter vacation in order to teach. Harvard and Bowdoin, which kept accurate records of such leaves, sent out about fifty teachers apiece every winter between 1800 and 1840, when enrollments ranged between 100 and 250. The American Education Society discovered the importance of schoolkeeping to its beneficiaries in 1827, when Elias Cornelius made a survey of the colleges. At Amherst, Bowdoin, Middlebury, Brown, and Dartmouth, all beneficiaries taught in the winter; at Williams, nine-tenths; at Waterville, the "largest part"; and at Yale, about half. Most of them taught at least three winters out of four, for about three months each year.[49] By the end of the eighteenth century, students who merely intended to go to college at some future time were taking jobs in small country schools, from exactly the same motives that prompted Ira Young and Mark Hopkins to do so. Samuel Austin (Yale, 1783) was among the earliest students at Yale to teach before enrolling in college.[50] Even in Mark Hopkins's day, a Yankee teacher who had not yet attended college was something of a novelty. "I have been several times asked at what College I was educated," Hopkins wrote his parents from his school in Virginia in 1820, "and surprise was indicated when I replied, at none."[51]

The scattered condition of the American school population in the nineteenth century made it impossible for students to teach school while living and studying in the college cloister. Occasionally, someone like Asa Turner, who taught near New Haven at Guilford, was able to commute between his work and his studies, but for the most part schoolkeeping scattered the young teachers into remote areas of the countryside, where they lived in intimate association with the families of their pupils.[52] Mark Hopkins boarded with the two families who hired him to keep school and was given his own cabin on the plantation grounds, sharing it occasionally with his scholars. In northern country schools, the teacher frequently lived and boarded a few days with each family, who treated him as a guest, not a servant.

His role as the teacher of children gave him a station quite different from that of a servant who waited on tables or kept petty records. If he mastered the problem of discipline, he became a figure of considerable authority and influence in the community. Moreover, his relationship to the college was different. He contracted with employers who had no connection with his college, and for the most part he supervised his own work. His income derived from the community in which he taught. In these respects, he had an understandable sense of independence and self-reliance, however hard his ordeal in a violent little country school might be.

At the same time, a young man who had controlled one of these schools came to college wiser and more mature than college boys in earlier years. Officials occasionally recognized this maturity, either by admitting a schoolkeeper to advanced standing or excusing his absences in term time. Samuel

Austin was among the first to gain advanced standing at Yale, probably because he had kept school and was older than a freshman ought to have been. President Stiles, who examined Austin on March 15, 1781, considered his admission to Yale as a sophomore extraordinary. "This is contrary to our general Rule," Stiles wrote in his diary, "but there were singular Reasons."[53] Mark Hopkins entered Williams as a sophomore in 1822, when advanced standing had become more common. Hopkins counted heavily on his maturity and self-preparation—acquired in part while teaching in Virginia—to win him a place among the sophomores.[54]

As the custom of keeping school became more common among undergraduates, the colleges reluctantly took account of it and provided for it. In 1749, after years of threatening to fine students who were absent in term time or charge them a fee for discontinuance, Harvard began to experiment with the calendar by creating the winter vacation so that poor scholars might leave for the long schoolkeeping season.[55] Other colleges—especially in New England—adopted this vacation and observed it for another century. Harvard, Amherst, and Williams maintained winter vacations of about five or six weeks until after midcentury. The policy at Harvard was typical.

> Meritorious Students, whose circumstances require it, may, at the discretion of the Faculty, be absent for a limited time, not exceeding thirteen weeks, including the winter vacation, for the purpose of keeping schools.[56]

The reluctance of officials to break up the college year was especially evident at Yale, where as late as 1782 the winter vacation lasted only from January 8 to January 29. This was far too short a period to take a school, though it is obvious from the diary of Ezra Stiles that some Yale students took their own long vacations.[57] None of the Yale catalogs in the nineteenth century advertised a long winter vacation or suggested that students might be absent in term time to keep school. Amherst attempted to reduce the winter vacation to two weeks in 1836, to conform with the policy at Yale, declaring that

> . . . much is inevitably lost to the student by the long vacation in winter, which was *formerly* a part of the arrangement. Such students as are obliged by their circumstances to teach school are allowed to be absent for the purpose; while *all the exercises* of the College are carried on just as if there were no such absence.[58]

Unfortunately, Amherst undertook this reform on the eve of a great depression, which only added to the difficulty of imposing such a calendar upon a student body that depended heavily upon schoolkeeping for income. In 1841 the college quietly reinstituted the winter recess, an inconvenience it had to endure for another thirty years.[59]

Presidents of the New England colleges had expressed their unanimous frustration at the persistence of schoolkeeping when the American Education Society polled them in 1827, but none of these men could offer a way to end it. The only alternatives were the old forms of manual labor required by farms

and shops. There probably had never been a time when some indigent students
in New England had not gone home for the planting or harvesting seasons
to help parents in the fields or to labor for a time with their hands. Toward
the end of the eighteenth century, a few colleges in America—especially those
in newly settled and sparsely populated areas—began to encourage students
to hire themselves out as laborers in the college community, to persons who
were not their parents. Eleazar Wheelock may have started this policy first,
during the early years of Dartmouth; Wheelock sent his students to work for
Hanover farmers, who provided them with board in return.[60] Students could
always find farm work near a provincial college; such work had the virtue
of keeping the poor gathered together through the year, though they might
leave for whole days. Like schoolkeeping, it required that students earn their
money outside the college. Between 1820 and 1840, advocates of the manual-
labor system tried to incorporate farms and shops into the colleges themselves,
but the movement never gained a wide following in New England except as
a physical culture program. Schoolkeeping undercut the economic advantages
of manual labor in densely populated New England, and officials were reluctant
to permit each day—as well as every academic year—to be interrupted by
periods of work.

When the collegiate community collapsed under the economic pressures
of the early nineteenth-century student population, so too did the old ideal
of a community of scholars secluded together under the same roofs. Rich and
poor separated, and the whole community dispersed. And while the social
classes no longer shared the same life or mixed so intensely at any New England college, the new arrangements did make it possible for a student society
of increasing variety and complexity to develop within these small institutions.
Choice and variety became qualities of student life, replacing the commonness
of experience when everyone had been gathered and secluded together, engaged
in the same studies at the same time. Fragmentation also introduced a crisis
of disorder. College officials found themselves subjected to pressures arising
within the colleges, and they were forced to abandon the old model of the
collegiate community—by now an anachronistic institution inherited from history—in favor of some new system for ordering life, a system that eventually
would assume a bureaucratic form.

Notes

1   Baxter P. Smith, *The History of Dartmouth
    College* (Boston: Houghton, Osgood and
    Company, 1878), pp. 290-91.
2   *Catalogue of the Officers and Students of
    Williams College, March, 1822* (n.p.,
    [1822]), pp. 5-8; *Catalogue of the Officers
    and Students of the Collegiate Institution,
    Amherst, Mass., Oct. 1822* (Greenfield,
    Mass.: Denio & Phelps, 1822), pp. 5-9. All
    nine students from Amherst were listed as
    having rooms in the college in 1822, sug-
    gesting how strongly the assumption still

prevailed that students would reside in college. As enrollment increased, however, it
became more common for town students to
live at home.
3   Emory Washburn, "Introduction," in Cal-
    vin Durfee, *A History of Williams College*
    (Boston: A. Williams and Company, 1860),
    pp. 20-21.
4   Julian Sturtevant, *Julian M. Sturtevant: An
    Autobiography*, ed. J. M. Sturtevant, Jr.
    (New York: F. H. Revell Company,
    [1896]), p. 73.

5 "The Lawes of the Colledge published publiquely before the Students of Harvard Colledge May 4, 1655," in Samuel Eliot Morison, ed., *Harvard College Records*, Publications of the Colonial Society of Massachusetts (Boston, 1935), 3:331, 341.

6 "College Book IV," *Harvard Records*, 2:520; Josiah Quincy, *The History of Harvard University*, 2 vols. (Cambridge, Mass.: John Owen, 1840), 2:95-96, 100; Benjamin Wadsworth, "Benjamin Wadsworth's Book," *Harvard Records*, 3:462, 493, 498-503; Louis L. Tucker, *Puritan Protagonist: President Thomas Clap of Yale College* (Chapel Hill: University of North Carolina Press, 1962), pp. 250-51; Beverly McAnear, "College Founding in the American Colonies, 1745-1775," *Mississippi Valley Historical Review* 42 (1955): 37. McAnear suggests that the college arrangements were cheaper, which may have been true for many students, but not for all.

7 These figures are based on admissions records in "Students Entering Harvard College, 1725-1832," and Records of the College Faculty, vols. 7 and 8, Harvard University Archives, Cambridge, Mass.; for Yale the sources are biographical data in Franklin B. Dexter, *Biographical Sketches of the Graduates of Yale College*, 6 vols. (New York and New Haven: Henry Holt and Company and Yale University Press, 1885-1912). At Yale the percentages of graduates over twenty-five years old were as follows: 9.9 percent in 1751-60; 13.0 percent in 1761-70; 16.5 percent in 1771-80; 10.2 percent in 1781-90; and 9.9 percent in 1791-1800.

8 Ezra Stiles, *The Literary Diary of Ezra Stiles*, ed. Franklin B. Dexter, 3 vols. (New York: Charles Scribner's Sons, 1901), 2:385, 428-29.

9 "College Book I," *Harvard Records*, 1:145-46, 148-51.

10 Ibid., pp. 141, 146.

11 The Harvard College orders of 1660 required students who chose to live in town to pay "detriments," a fee to compensate the college for loss of revenue. In 1725 Harvard required students who received exhibitions and who resided in the college to dine in commons, which suggests that poor students already were finding cheaper board in the town. See "College Book III," *Harvard Records*, 1:192; "College Book IV," ibid., 2:519.

12 Sturtevant, *Sturtevant*, pp. 78-80.

13 William R. Thayer, "History and Customs of Harvard University," in *Universities and Their Sons*, ed. Joshua L. Chamberlain, 5 vols. (Boston: R. Herndon Company, 1898-1900), 1:164.

14 This is Samuel Eliot Morison's interpretation of evidence in stewards' records; see Morison, *Harvard College in the Seventeenth Century*, 2 vols. (Cambridge, Mass.: Harvard University Press, 1936), 1:100.

15 Quincy, *Harvard*, 2:98.

16 Robert S. Rait, *The Universities of Aberdeen: A History* (Aberdeen, Scotland: James Gordon Bisset, 1895), p. 204. See also W. M. Mathew, "The Origins and Occupations of Glasgow Students, 1740-1839," *Past and Present*, no. 33 (1966), pp. 74-94.

17 *Catalogue of the Officers and Students in Yale College, November, 1827* ([New Haven]: Treadway and Adams, 1827), p. 28.

18 Quincy, *Harvard*, 2:359-60, 560.

19 *Catalogue of the Officers and Students in Yale College, 1844-45* (New Haven: B. L. Hamlen, 1844), p. 33.

20 Thayer, "Harvard," pp. 166; Samuel Eliot Morison, *Three Centuries of Harvard, 1636-1936* (Cambridge, Mass.: Harvard University Press, 1936), pp. 251, 312.

21 Thomas Chapman, "Journal of a Tourist Through the Eastern States, 1796," *Historical Magazine*, 2d ser. 7 (1870): 17. The Yale catalog for 1855-56 cited these rules: "No student is allowed to be a boarder in any hotel or house of public entertainment in the city of New Haven. . . . The students living out of College are not allowed to room in any house or building, in which a family does not reside." *Catalogue of the Officers and Students in Yale College, 1855-56* (New Haven: Ezekiel Hayes, 1855), pp. 42-43. Harvard had comparable rules.

22 Mark Hopkins, *Early Letters of Mark Hopkins*, ed. S. S. H. (New York: John Day Company, 1929), p. 92.

23 *Catalogue of Williams, 1822*, p. 12.

24 Hopkins, *Early Letters*, p. 102.

25 Quoted in William S. Tyler, *History of Amherst College During Its First Half Century, 1821-1871* (Springfield, Mass.: Clark W. Bryan and Company, 1873), p. 80.

26 Evidence regarding the greater expense of dining in families comes from the early nineteenth-century college catalogs of Harvard, Amherst, Yale, Williams, Bowdoin, and Dartmouth.

27 The first reference to private boardinghouses in the Yale catalog appears in the edition of 1841-42, although they existed before the catalog took notice of them. See *Catalogue of the Officers and Students in Yale College, 1841-42* (New Haven: B. L. Hamlen, 1841), p. 31.

28 William G. Hammond, *Remembrance of Amherst: An Undergraduate's Diary, 1846-1848*, ed. George F. Whicher (New York: Columbia University Press, 1946), pp. 23-24.

29 Quoted in Louis C. Hatch, *The History of Bowdoin College* (Portland, Me.: Loring, Short & Harmon, 1927), p. 227.

30 *Catalogue of the Officers and Students in*

Yale College, 1839-40 (New Haven: B. L. Hamlen, 1839), p. 31; *Catalogue of Yale, 1841-42*, p. 31; *Catalogue of the Officers and Students of Amherst College, for the Academical Year 1842-43* (Amherst, Mass.: J. S. & C. Adams, [1842]), p. 19.

31 *Catalogue of Yale, 1827-28*, p. 28.

32 Washburn, "Introduction," pp. 21-22.

33 Quoted in Tyler, *Amherst*, pp. 75, 79.

34 This account of college rooms is based on the early nineteenth-century catalogs of Williams, Amherst, Yale, Harvard, Bowdoin, Middlebury, Vermont, and Dartmouth.

35 Charles Bristed, *Five Years in an English University*, 2d ed. (New York: G. P. Putnam & Co., 1852), pp. 425-26; *Catalogue of the Officers and Students in Yale College, 1856-57* (New Haven: Ezekiel Hayes, 1856), p. 34; *Catalogue of the Officers and Students of Amherst College, for the Academical Year 1858-59* (Amherst, Mass.: John H. Brewster, 1858), pp. 24-25; *Harvard University Catalogue, 1889-90* (Cambridge, Mass.: Harvard University, 1889), pp. 165-66; *Catalogue of Yale University, 1889-90* (New Haven: Tuttle, Morehouse & Taylor, 1889), pp. 63-64.

36 Evidence for town rooms is taken from the same group of early nineteenth-century catalogs. All these catalogs quoted prices of rooms in town, beginning about 1840.

37 See the college catalogs for these years.

38 This conclusion is based on a study of the college residences of A.E.S. beneficiaries listed in A.E.S. records and the catalogs.

39 *Catalogue of Yale, 1827-28*, pp. 11-22; *Catalogue of the Officers and Students in Yale College, 1850-51* (New Haven: B. L. Hamlen, 1850), pp. 14-28.

40 For a discussion of these forms of work, see Philippe Aries, *Centuries of Childhood: A Social History of Family Life*, trans. Robert Baldick (New York: Alfred A. Knopf, 1962), p. 367.

41 *Catalogue of the Officers and Students of Yale College, November, 1822* (New Haven: A. H. Maltby & Co., 1822), p. 27. Similar provisions appeared in the records and laws of Harvard College until the same decade.

42 See the Yale laws of 1745 in Franklin B. Dexter, *Biographical Sketches of the Graduates of Yale College*, vol. 2 (New York: Henry Holt and Company, 1896), pp. 13-14; see also the regular references to stu-

dent labor in the four "College Books," *Harvard Records*.

43 See the Yale laws of 1726 in Dexter, *Graduates of Yale*, vol. 1 (New York: Henry Holt and Company, 1885), p. 347.

44 Dexter, *Graduates of Yale*, 2:14-15.

45 Quincy, *Harvard*, 2:561-62.

46 Account Book of Theophilus Packard (copy), Amherst College Archives, Amherst, Mass.; original in Packard Family Papers, Bancroft Library, University of California, Berkeley, Calif.

47 Account Book of Daniel Bliss, Amherst Archives.

48 Clifford K. Shipton, *Sibley's Harvard Graduates*, vol. 4 (Cambridge, Mass.: Harvard University Press, 1933), pp. 398-99.

49 Elias Cornelius to Francis Wayland, January 18, 1830, Letter Book 1, American Education Society Archives, Congregational Library, Boston, Mass.

50 Dexter, *Graduates of Yale*, vol. 4 (New York: Henry Holt and Company, 1907), pp. 248-57.

51 Hopkins, *Early Letters*, p. 61.

52 George F. Magoun, *Asa Turner: A Home Missionary Patriarch and His Times* (Boston: Congregational Sunday-School and Publishing Society, [1889]), pp. 45-46. John Todd took a school two and one-half miles from Yale in the winter of 1818-19. He walked back and forth every day. See John Todd, ed., *John Todd: The Story of His Life, Told Mainly by Himself* (New York: Harper & Brothers, 1876), pp. 68-69.

53 Stiles, *Diary*, 2:522; Dexter, *Graduates of Yale*, 4:248-57.

54 Hopkins, *Early Letters*, p. 75.

55 "College Book IV," *Harvard Records*, 2:807.

56 *Catalogue of the Officers and Students of Harvard College, for the Academical Year 1850-51*, 1st term, 2d ed. (Cambridge, Mass.: Metcalf and Company, 1850), p. 81.

57 Stiles, *Diary*, 3:2, 5-7.

58 *Catalogue of the Officers and Students [of Amherst College], November, 1836* (Amherst, Mass.: J. S. & C. Adams, 1836), p. 18.

59 *Catalogue of the Officers and Students of Amherst College, for the Academical Year 1841-42* (Amherst, Mass.: J. S. & C. Adams, [1841]), p. 19.

60 McAnear, "College Founding," p. 32.

7 The Dangers of Antebellum Student Life

We merely desire you to know what dangers attend College life.

Amherst College Faculty, 1845

Old ways of ordering daily existence within the collegiate community came into conflict with a changing style of student life in the early nineteenth century. In the course of half a century, New England students began to experience a liberation surpassing all known precedents, involving greater independence and sociability than the old collegiate community had permitted. Disorder now appeared, both as a kind of intimate anarchy in daily personal behavior and also in the form of collective rebellions and riots. Professors and presidents confronted a student population whose behavior at every level was passing beyond their control.

The disarray of personal lives revealed itself in the diaries and letters that the students wrote. Such personal documents, covering large segments of whole student careers, have survived for a few students at every New England college. Those left by four students at Amherst College between 1820 and 1850 disclose the most striking, typical features of the new style of life: its independence, its dense social commerce between students and society, and its ever present need for self-discipline.

Story Hebard, of the class of 1828, entered Amherst from Lebanon, New Hampshire, in the fall of 1824 at age twenty-two. When he wrote his first letter home, on October 25, 1824, he had already assumed the regulation of his own time. Studies absorbed only seven prescribed hours of his day—from

9:00 A.M. to noon, from 2:00 P.M. to 4:00 P.M., and from 7:00 P.M. to 9:00
P.M. In this time he attended classes and finished his lessons; "the remaining
part of the day I have to myself to do with it as I please."[1] When Josiah
Cary first came to the Amherst area in 1827 as an academy student, he and
his friends had to regulate their own hours of study in the boardinghouse. Cary
left his home in Brookfield just before his fourteenth birthday, when he began
his diary. At fifteen, he entered the college, where he spent his days in self-
reliance until graduation in 1832. William Hammond, class of 1849, Newport,
Rhode Island, left a diary for the years 1846-48 showing that life in the college
had retained these qualities down to midcentury.[2]

At Amherst, the college commanded only the hours of worship, recitation,
and lecture; the evening study period really had no supervision. Students necessarily established their own routines outside the classroom, even when they
roomed in college. For them, the allotment of time had become problematic,
no longer determined by the rhythms of a uniform, institutional routine, but
by themselves. Liberty demanded more self-discipline than most young men
could summon, however; disorderliness became a worrisome concern among
students themselves. Josiah Cary's friends at Amherst Academy formed their
own "early-rising society" in 1828 to help one another get out of bed. These
mutual-aid societies continued to form spontaneously throughout the 1820s and
1830s at Amherst, at both the college and the academies. John Farwell, of
the class of 1836, joined one in 1833. "We aim to retire at ten, & rise at
five—so far I believe we have more than done it," he wrote to his sister.
In 1835 Farwell was having less success on his own.

> I have had no regular system in the appropriation of my time, since my
> return to col. but have "lived altogether extempore"—sometimes sitting
> up rather late, & generally keeping my bed till the bell rings, a thing I
> have never practiced before since I have been here: nor do I intend to
> follow it now.

Farwell knew that others were having the same trouble; they generally observed
morning duties, but institutional restraints faded with the day. One "friend
of good order," who preferred to remain anonymous, beseeched the faculty
in 1829 to intervene "when students spend almost whole knights in roasting
and eating turkeys potatoes &c, . . . and when too they absolutely get drunk,
when the name of God is taken in vain without the least restraint, when students repeatedly take supper at a public house in the village &c &c &c &c."[3]
With no commons at Amherst, once the college permitted students to find
rooms in the village beginning in the late 1820s, the young men then controlled
options formerly in the hands of officials. Though the faculty restricted students
to approved boardinghouses and rooming houses, student prerogative asserted
itself. Story Hebard, Josiah Cary, and William Hammond all shifted their
places of board and room at will. Rarely did the faculty control these decisions.

Seclusion disappeared from the lives of these students at early Amherst,
as it did elsewhere in New England. Between 1800 and 1860 there began to
rise an irrepressible sociability between New England students and towns-

people, a mixing in daily life, leisure, and local controversy that only exceptional individuals had experienced in colonial New Haven and Cambridge.
Young men who found neither food, lodging, nor work within the college simply could not be restrained from entering the life of the adult society around
them. Amherst students and citizens negotiated with one another over board
and room; they lived together in the same houses, forming ties of intimacy.
"It has been my lot to be placed in a family so agreeable that I scarcely know
or perceive sometimes whether I am at home or among strangers," wrote Story
Hebard from Mrs. Montague's house in 1825. "Nothing is too good for me
which the house affords and if I am the least out of health I have all the
attention which I could possibly need." Nor could the faculty confine student-
community relations to matters concerning board and room, though they tried.
In the spring of 1832 they admonished townspeople for furnishing "means
of indulgence and dissipation to the students" at Gilbert's hotel; later in the
year they had to deny students access to Hatfield's grocery for any purpose
whatsoever.[4]

Amherst was a hive for indigent students, whose gathering within a small
village compounded the difficulties of secluding them. Poverty itself demanded
commerce with the society. Work removed students from college and carried
them into the community as teachers in common schools, singing schools, Sunday schools—where they entered local churches—or as traveling agents, selling
books or preaching and raising funds in the country around the village. A letter
from Story Hebard to his brother suggests how roles were played in securing
a job: "I determined to engage it, consulted the President & obtained permission." The swarming of indigent young men at Amherst forced students like
Hebard to search farther and farther from college for schools to keep. On one
occasion in 1824 he left town for two days, just looking for a school; President
Humphrey discovered an opening for him 150 miles away. In 1825 Hebard
taught in New Jersey, and in 1826 and 1827 he taught common school and
singing in Worcester County. Hence, the propensity for travel among antebellum students. And since they spent vacations on their own—away both from
school and family—their college years became a time of socializing, not seclusion.[5]

The student career of John Farwell may explain why Amherst College fostered this kind of life and why that institution inevitably was drawn from its
seclusion into the very social controversies that it sought most to avoid. Farwell
was nearly twenty-four when he enrolled at Amherst in February 1833; he
was already a teacher of some experience, having delayed his higher education
because of poverty. He came to Amherst from Ashby, Massachusetts, as a
beneficiary of the American Education Society; already he had committed himself to the cause of evangelical Christianity. "We hope for a revival," he
wrote in his first letter from college. His religious work began at once, both
in college and town: "Attended a social prayermeeting this evening which was
nearly as interesting as ever I knew."

Josiah Cary had attended meetings like these at Amherst in the 1820s, and
when Story Hebard was a tutor in 1831, he witnessed a "Three Days Meeting"
in a village church that drew crowds of 500-600 persons, including both stu-

dents and townspeople. Farwell and a classmate assisted the temporary minister in the south parish of Amherst for at least nine consecutive weeks in 1836, when the church needed help at the third Sabbath exercise.[6] He soon came to believe that he had a special duty to evangelize his family, and he felt obligations as a student to promote reform in the community. After one vacation in his early career at Amherst, he confessed to his sister that he wanted to do more.

> It seems to me when I glance backward from the occurrences of last winter, as if I had been spellbound or bewildered, all the time I was at home. I did nothing as I intended before I left college. In my school—in the neighborhood, the social circle, at home I was anything rather than the example of ardent, humble piety, which my duty required, & which you all might have reasonably expected.[7]

Neither his maturity nor his poverty and piety made John Farwell exceptional among Amherst students. Indeed, the college had sought such students, especially among beneficiaries of the American Education Society. In doing this, it had attracted young men like Farwell, already stirred by revivals and reform at home, who brought their commitments with them. Given a society that was stirring the commitments and politicizing the lives of young men, and given the dense commerce of students with that society, there was no way for Amherst College to prevent the tensions of New England from intruding upon its seclusion.

John Farwell may have become an abolitionist as late as a year and a half after his arrival at Amherst. He may have caught this enthusiasm, in other words, within the college itself, where Southerners also had begun to enroll. In early July 1834, he first mentioned to his sister that he had attended a meeting of the County Colonization Society—perhaps in the village of Templeton, some thirty miles eastward in Worcester County—where a mixed group of students and citizens heard a talk by John Todd. By December 14, 1834, at the very latest, Farwell had become an advocate of immediate abolition. He had taken a winter school at Groton, Massachusetts, to which town he carried his convictions. He boarded with two sisters and their bachelor brother, a sociable family. "They are all, moreover, thoroughly steeped in the spirit of Anti Slavery, & in truth we talk little else," he wrote to his sister.[8] In February 1835, as he traveled back to Amherst from his schoolkeeping, he began the kind of agitation soon to disrupt whole communities and bring violence even to the college.

> About 10. o clock I started for Waltons tavern where I passed the night & the next morn came on, as I expected to Amherst. With my usual garrulity, I talked Abolition or temperance most of the way: I found just enough opposition to enliven conversation &c. &c. &c. &c.[9]

It was probably some of Farwell's fellow students, members of the Amherst Auxiliary Anti-Slavery Society, who converted him to abolition. The society

TABLE 8   Graduation Ages of Abolitionists at Amherst College, 1834-35
(78 Members)

Ages	19	20	21	22	23	24	25	26	27	28	29	30	?
Number of students		2	5	3	13	2	12	8	7	11	5	4	3 3

Note: The years refer to dates of the society, not to graduating classes.

had formed during a "great excitement" in July 1833, in opposition to a student Colonization Society founded a few weeks earlier. It started slowly, according to the abolitionists' own account. "Publick opinion was entirely against us. Only *eight* or ten individuals *dared* to avow themselves Abolitionists." By October 1834, seventy-eight students had been connected with the society, about one-fourth of the enrollment; all but six of these were declared to be "professors of religion." John Farwell, whose signature is thirty-sixth on the membership list, had to have been a member by this date.[10]

Like most Amherst students, these abolitionists were poor young men—hardly members of a displaced elite. Almost exactly half of them were, like Farwell, beneficiaries of the American Education Society. Also like most Amherst students, they were mature young men, as typically mature as the student abolitionists that Theodore Dwight Weld was gathering in the West; more than two-thirds of the original seventy-eight members were over twenty-four years old at graduation.[11] Farwell was nearly twenty-seven. The full range of their ages was equally typical (see Table 8).

This society sprang spontaneously from within the college, from impulses generated on campus but fed by the myriad private experiences of the students. It was not the product of outside organizations or the urge to imitate other societies. It began almost a year before the Lane debates. An antislavery group had formed at Williams College in 1823—the first in Massachusetts—but it had committed itself to gradual colonization. Theodore Dwight Weld had been working with students in the West as early as 1831, and antislavery societies started at Dartmouth and Bowdoin in 1835, drawing some inspiration (as well as members, in the case of Dartmouth) from student abolitionists in the academy and seminary at Andover. As late as February 1835, however, the Amherst faculty did not know that such student societies existed in any "respectable College but our own," though they did mention the Andover group. There is no evidence that Weld or the New England student groups had any influence among Amherst abolitionists.[12]

In regard to this abolitionism, these students were both teachers and petitioners, at first identifying the adult community as the audience for their message. They pledged to help in "the noble work of enlightening and educating the coloured population in our own vicinity and abroad," much as Weld's friends were doing in Cincinnati. In November 1834, they joined efforts to bring the slavery issue before Congress, voting "that those members of the

Society, who may be absent during the winter from College, be requested to make exertions in behalf of petitioning for the same object." It may have been in observance of this resolution that John Farwell talked abolition as he returned from Groton.

These activities brought conflict to the college. In February 1834, the society resolved "that all violent criminations, or harsh epithets applied to our opponents be considered ungentlemanly." Students were dividing against students over social issues. In the fall of 1834, after the Lane debates, President Heman Humphrey of Amherst urged the society to disband. The students refused; the President insisted. He spoke for the faculty: "We still believe that your own best good, & the permanent interests of the institution would be promoted by the voluntary disbanding of the Society." Humphrey and the faculty then moved to suppress the disorder; by the end of February 1835, the society had been dissolved.[13] The agitation does not appear to have subsided, however. "Feel as much interested in AntiSlavery as ever," John Farwell wrote in June. "Perhaps somewhat fanatical, but no matter. We do nothing about it here except pay our monthly subscriptions & talk among ourselves."[14]

On commencement morning in August, this quiet talk gave way to a moment of violence, a beating inflicted upon a Yankee by a Tennesseean "with a heavy cane." Robert C. McNairy of Nashville, Tennessee, was expelled; his victim, John Langdon Ashby of Bradford, New Hampshire, appears not to have belonged to the auxiliary, but the incident revived the antislavery movement at Amherst for a time. In 1836 the faculty permitted a second Anti-Slavery Society to form, this one not to become an auxiliary of any larger society.[15] Debaters were to join this group, making it much like the literary societies, except that it kept controversy before its members and within the college. Each monthly meeting attracted about thirty students; 103 members joined between 1837 and 1841, thirty-nine of them A.E.S. beneficiaries. They seldom operated outside the college, distinguishing themselves in this way from their predecessors and from some modern student movements of the twentieth century. With only three exceptions, all the members of this second group of antislavery students had graduated by September 1844. Their records cease abruptly in 1841; perhaps they saw no purpose in continuing in this fashion. One could always debate in the other societies or join a real antislavery group outside the college. And the faculty had learned to censor the politics out of commencement orations by this time.[16] Limits like these effectively suppressed the source of the most dangerous disorder and involvement.

It would be misleading to conclude that the social involvement engaged in by John Farwell, or even Josiah Cary and Story Hebard, ever became an accepted way of student life. There was no period of sanctioned involvement at antebellum colleges; the institutional setting that demanded that students mix in adult society and assume adult responsibilities never developed freely, without resistance from officials. Faculties strained to apply the old conception of collegiate discipline, *in loco parentis*, inhibiting by their willful adherence to an old ideology the growth of a student culture appropriate to new conditions. Their suppression of student antislavery societies represented only the most sensational effort on their part to preserve the old order. The parental conception of discipline through seclusion survived in college legal codes, despite revisions in language and detail, until after the Civil War. Custom kept these codes alive, since few could yet imagine a better way to govern. At Amherst, even though none of the institutions to sustain such a code existed, the first laws of 1822 imposed a regime that was traditional in every respect: the same listing of crimes and punishments, the same powers of government and discipline handed to the faculty—except that they could not require a student to live in any specific place. Even the language was reminiscent of the earliest Harvard laws; it imposed a parental role upon the Amherst faculty.

> It shall be the duty of the Faculty diligently to inspect and watch over the manners and behaviour of the students, and in all proper methods, both by example and precept to recommend to them a virtuous and blameless life, and a diligent attention to the public and private duties of religion.[17]

They kept the old ways of inspecting and watching: student monitors to mark absences, tutors to reside in college buildings and observe behavior, officers to visit rooms. They took it all seriously, too. "Scholars are prohibited by the laws of College to be seen out of their rooms during any study hours," wrote Benjamin Cressy from Amherst in 1822, "and not infrequently do some of the officers come and peek into our rooms, to see if we are at home and studying as we ought to be." Francis Wayland revived an even older system of supervision after he became president of Brown in 1826, requiring officers actually to occupy apartments in college "during the day and evening," and to "visit the rooms of students at least twice during the twenty-four hours."[18]

Even as these laws were being written or copied, however, they had become quaint. Familial analogies once used to describe relations between teachers and students no longer applied very well. Story Hebard sincerely tried to think of himself as a child—at least he tried to use the metaphor—in describing a college dinner at the end of the summer term in 1828. Everyone gathered at President Humphrey's house. "The President was quite social, related many interesting anecdotes, and gave us much good advise for the future—He calls us all his children, and we are proud to own him as our Father." Yet Humphrey was an old fool if he took this seriously. To his "child," Hebard, the whole occasion seemed old-fashioned and quite beyond the context of ordinary experience at Amherst.

> It made me think of good old Thanks-Giving times, when children are permitted, after an absence of some days, months, or years, to return to their native home, and their parents have the unspeakable pleasure of seeing their little family circle complete and happy.[19]

When John C. Adams and Chauncey A. Hall of the class of 1833 were fined fifty cents each for attending services at the village church, they employed the analogy only to twist it. They acknowledged the "claim" of the faculty "to hold the same relation to us that a father does to his son." Then they let it be known that the young could invoke both metaphor and scripture to deliver a warning: "Fathers, provoke not your children to wrath."[20]

This initial response to the disorder of antebellum student life, this effort to preserve the tone and substance of parental discipline, failed. The mere attempt to enforce old laws now led to innovation; it took energy without giving order in return. And—it did not work. As students scattered and professors moved away from residence halls, visitation lost its air of casual, personal attentiveness and revealed itself as a form of police detection. Faculty minutes are rife with confessions of failure. In 1830 the Amherst faculty determined "that a more efficient system of inspection of the students be adopted immediately," with officers to visit assigned rooms twice a week. They next resolved—and then rescinded their resolution—to fine any officer who neglected his visits. In 1831 they extended visitation to rooms in the village, making it a special duty of Professor Hitchcock.[21]

Student diaries and memoirs indicate that visits did take place, though they were described as "special occasions."[22] Periodically, the faculty declared its intention to perform this duty, suggesting that visitation waxed and waned. It uncovered no significant lawlessness; rarely did Amherst enter upon its records a crime detected through visitation. Rumor apprised the faculty of student excursions to Northampton; students themselves reported thefts, assaults, and disturbances in the halls; landladies and physicians informed the college of fornication.

Faculty observation really prevailed only at chapel and in the classroom, and even here officials were vexed by the ineptitude and cowardice of student monitors. Since students traveled frequently, officers could not always be certain to find an individual at any given time. So, in the fall of 1825, the Amherst faculty procured a massive Register book, in which they proposed to enter every departure, arrival, and excuse—an old device employed even in the eighteenth century. This measure at Amherst now produced new difficulties. Some students did indeed register (their names rapidly filling the book), but many did not. Such neglect (a new offense) had to be discovered and punished. Every scheme entailed more work and dragged the faculty into mounting conflict with the students.[23]

It was only in the small rooming houses, where students lived with real families in private homes, that a kind of family discipline prevailed. Here a student might find privacy, with perhaps a greater liberty to smoke and regulate his own hours, since he could move his lodgings at will; but his existence while actually in the house was scarcely bohemian. His life would assume the kind of order known to any young adult in a nineteenth-century family, more order than residents in the college might find. "I room out of College because I am more retired & have a better opportunity for study," Story Hebard explained to his brother in 1824. Within the college residence halls, if there was order, it was students who kept it. Vigilantes supported the law at Yale in Julian Sturtevant's days. Amherst created a student government in 1828 to police the college, the first such experiment in New England; in 1830 the students voted to abolish it.[24] The temperance societies that formed in the late 1820s—the early-rising societies—all sprang from a recognition by students that, ultimately, only mutual aid and self-discipline could impose order when institutional regulation had weakened.

In all the writing on college life of the early nineteenth century, there emerged a sensitivity to disorder, a sense that student society had passed beyond the grasp of old authority and taken on the aspect of bohemianism. "Hardly any class of men are so difficult to be reached as students, and the undertaking is hazardous," wrote John Todd, prefacing *The Student's Manual* he published in 1835. Four comparable manuals for students appeared between 1830 and 1837 in New England alone, reviving an ancient genre and rousing a new concern for the way students were living. Perhaps as few as five comparable books had been published in all America before this time; the form almost had disappeared.[25]

Where handbooks of the eighteenth century had been written under the assumption that students needed information about the curriculum, advice on study, deportment, manners, and conversation—together with a few admonitions on conduct—those of the 1830s became books of caution, addressing the dangers of antebellum student life. A new emphasis on disorderliness worked its way into the most conventional of the new works and prevented them from becoming mere copies of their predecessors. John Todd borrowed whole passages from John Mason's *The Student and Pastor*, an English work first printed in America in 1794, but Todd had new purposes. He offered all the conventional advice and more; employing a metaphor common to the new books, he sought to "shield" youth from danger.[26]

The dangers identified by authors of the 1830s all proceeded from areas of student life where institutional controls had been removed by the demise of the collegiate community, where students themselves were having to make decisions governing their daily affairs. Edward Hitchcock's *Dyspepsy Forestalled & Resisted* (1830) addressed the consequences of an institutional void in regimen: colleges were relinquishing responsibilities for the student's board, and they had not yet assumed the supervision of his health. The student lived without family restraints or collegiate custom, a potential victim of his own ignorance or intemperance. Asa Dodge Smith, in *Letters to a Young Student* (1832), expressed new fears of sociability in antebellum student life. Scattered through his bits of conventional wisdom, readers found precautions about the liberties of boardinghouse life, warnings against visiting and mingling with the populace during the day or at special seasons of revivals. William Cogswell's *Letters to Young Men Preparing for the Christian Ministry* (1837) expressed identical fears of student "intercourse with the world" while the young men were teaching and traveling.[27]

It was not difficult for John Todd to imagine a total disintegration of personal and collective order at college. His imagination drove him to improve upon the eighteenth-century manuals that served as his models but that did not reflect his new fears. Where John Mason, in *The Student and Pastor* (1794), had called dutifully, but briefly, for "the regulation of appetites and passions," Todd interrupted even his chapter on reading to warn—in three pages of Latin—against onanism, the ultimate expression of personal disorder. John Clarke had included only a passing remark about "riotous actions within the walls of the college" in *Letters to a Student* (1796); Todd composed a whole section on the evils of student rebellion, taking almost enough space for a new chapter.[28]

Each of the new works was in fact a manual of discipline, imposing order on the most minute activities of each day. Hitchcock demanded total abstinence from both sexual relations and alcohol; he prescribed a simple diet suited to the needs of indigent students, urging them at the same time to form experimental boarding clubs like those at Amherst, where solitary individuals might find strength in the discipline of group regimen. His instructions on sleeping, rising, evacuating the bowels, exercising, bathing, and dressing surpassed conventional advice on these matters; behind each rule stood Hitchcock's assumption that health and achievement in student life now depended on self-regulation. Smith, Todd, and Cogswell adopted Hitchcock's doctrines but relied more heavily on traditional restraints of religion to provide order in a student's existence. Smith urged his readers to select only Christian roommates and companions. "In view of the duties and dangers of college life," he wrote, "look up for help to Him, who alone can make you strong for every duty, and shield you from every danger."[29]

Mere conventions of cautionary literature did not produce these fears and warnings; they cannot be dismissed as the exaggerations of scribblers. Each of these men had professional connections with higher education. Hitchcock was professor of chemistry and natural history at Amherst in 1830, later becoming president. Smith had graduated from Dartmouth in 1830 and was still a student at Andover Theological Seminary when he wrote his manual; he was soon to become a professor, and later president, at Dartmouth. John Todd, in 1835 a minister at Northampton, had left Yale only a dozen years earlier and had become a favorite speaker at Amherst College. William Cogswell probably learned more about the New England student population than any of the others through his work as secretary of the American Education Society. The authors spoke with authority about conditions in collegiate institutions.

Identical fears were being voiced within the colleges themselves after 1830. In about 1840 members of the Amherst faculty began to lecture students on college life, complementing the influence of published manuals; other faculties came to follow the same practice. It was when faculties began to address the *families* of students that the depth of these fears was revealed. "We merely desire you to know what dangers attend College life," wrote the Amherst faculty in their first circular letter to parents in 1845. There followed a confession of maddening disorders. Students would depart from college during term time without excuse. Their schoolkeeping deranged scholarship, health, and academic exercises. They practiced habits "unfavorable to study and morality," despite the presence of Hitchcock himself; drinking persisted and smoking had become more common. They rode out of town frequently. "Eminently injurious are such excursions when they are undertaken, as they often are, at night." Student sociability had escaped all bounds, giving rise to "social and convivial gatherings" wherever young men wanted to meet—in restaurants, groceries, taverns, and places providing "secret apartments, where the grossest dissipation may be indulged undiscovered."[30]

These fears cannot be dismissed as the ludicrous inventions and stock responses of puritanical authorities who always saw evil in the unchanging impulses of youth and tried to repress those impulses with harsh standards of discipline. For the first time, the Amherst faculty was confessing, before the very parents whose sons they supervised, their inability to maintain order. The faculty was calling for help, admitting its "own insufficiency" and owning up to its need "not only of parental aid, but of wisdom from on high." This confession had neither the confident tone one might find in an assertion of old standards nor the unquestioning attitude of a stock response. The fears it expressed in common with the handbooks of the 1830s—fears of a totally undisciplined student culture—had not appeared in earlier literature on student life with such urgency. Real troubles had developed within these institutions, troubles that were insurmountable by any methods yet known in the early nineteenth century. A new sensibility was emerging here, fearful and intolerant of disorder.

Traces of this intolerance appeared early in the nineteenth century. College disciplinary records between 1800 and 1830 reveal a rising preoccupation with disorder in everyday, personal affairs. Little notebooks like those kept by President Clap at Yale in the eighteenth century gave way to heavy ledgers, as infractions once minimized by collegiate routines and treated in personal consultations now became more frequent, subject only to forms of control that inevitably were becoming more bureaucratic. Faculties became increasingly intolerant of disorder, even in minor matters.

During the academic year 1830-31, the Amherst faculty acted on at least eighty-nine different cases of discipline in its regular meetings. Three cases involved intoxication; three involved absences without leave; four involved poor scholarship. One dealt with insubordination, four with misconduct, and only eight involved actual disturbances of the peace. Sixty-six cases involved violations of prescribed college routine, a portion typical for collegiate institutions in these years and an indication of the kind of concerns upon which faculties were fixing their attention. Whole faculty meetings were consumed in dealing with violations of college law, until faculties were gathering for almost no other purpose. President Bennet Tyler of Dartmouth complained in 1828 that disciplinary matters were taking more time than "any person without experience would be likely to imagine."[31] Their energies were absorbed with small infractions, manifestations of personal disorder.

More spectacular forms of disorder accompanied these distractions. In the middle of the eighteenth century, collective acts of rational, purposeful violence and organized rebellion began to appear amid the eternal pranks of students at Harvard and Yale. These incidents represented a change in the form of student group behavior, a change that persisted into the nineteenth century, increasing in frequency between 1820 and 1850. All the rebellions and incidents of student mobs between 1760 and 1860 should be placed in this context of a rising curve of collective student disorder.

Between 1760 and 1860 New England colleges experienced the most rebellious century in their history. Yale's troubles escalated into a ten-year rebellion against President Clap's "confounded arbitrary Government" between 1756 and 1766. Harvard recorded its first rebellion in 1766; others followed in 1768, 1780, and 1805. Students at Brown rebelled against college officers in 1798 and 1800; Williams experienced its first "insurrection against the government of the College" in 1802, then another in 1808.[32] Between 1820 and 1860 these small New England institutions confronted almost universal disquietude.

Harvard encountered "extraordinary resistance" to college government between 1818 and 1823, causing its overseers to summon the faculty to explain the status of discipline in Cambridge. At Brown, "deliberate, organized, and protracted" rebellions between 1824 and 1826 forced a president to resign. Between 1820 and 1850, Harvard, Yale, Brown, Dartmouth, Bowdoin, Middlebury, Amherst, and Vermont all experienced at least one incident of organized violence or rebellion, and their discipline records indicate an annual incidence of collective lawlessness on the part of small numbers of students.[33] The action of these small mobs usually was directed against specific students or faculty members and against college property; only rarely did these incidents assume the character of jokes or pranks.

Individual acts of violence and terrorism disrupted order in residence halls with what appears to have been increasing frequency beginning in the 1820s. "The fall term of the college year, 1823-24, was marked by great disturbances and many deeds of violence," wrote Julian Sturtevant, recalling his years in the class of 1826—a class that witnessed the bombing of a residence hall. "As I think of it at this distance, it seems almost incredible that the body of students should have been so deeply imbued with the spirit of hostility to the college government."[34]

In terms of scale, the disorder at Yale exceeded all others in New England and America before the twentieth century. Yale students carried arms; a tutor died of stab wounds in 1843. In the town-gown riots of 1841, 1854, and 1858, students fought New Haven firemen in street battles, one of which involved a crowd of 1,200 to 1,500 persons. Students barricaded themselves in the college. In each of the last two riots, firemen were shot to death by students. City and college officials in New Haven could expect town-gown riots to recur at any time during the 1840s and 1850s. Also at Yale, where southern students enrolled in large numbers, memoirs from the antebellum decades suggest that miniature civil wars erupted over ideological and sectional issues, creating a constant source of internal conflict, though surviving records make it difficult to draw ideological lines precisely between Northerners and Southerners. On at least two occasions, small groups of Yale students disrupted antislavery meetings in the town.[35]

Given the exceptional defiance and lawlessness of students after 1760, it is tempting to explain the rise of collective disorder in terms comparable to modern experience. The unrest of the eighteenth century could be viewed as the product of ideology associated with the Revolution, with students challenging authority and gaining rights. The unrest before the Civil War could be related to the rise of organized antislavery movements. In either case, disorder might be explained as the product of student movements employing ideas having currency in adult society. Or, in the case of antebellum students, unrest might be explained as the product of a peculiarly disturbed and violent generation that was responding to forces of change that were restructuring American society and creating fear and opposition among the population of widely scattered communities.

Yet these explanations do not account fully for the various forms of disorder, or for faculty fears and reaction. It was not violence, really, that roused faculty fears; spectacular rebellion was not central to all the disorders, nor does it explain the reaction that followed. The riots and rebellions occurred too sporadically to have had a continuing impact on any single institution, with the possible exceptions of Harvard and Yale at certain periods. More isolated and localized than the student rebellions of the 1960s, involving far fewer numbers of students, these collective disturbances did not lead faculties to perceive themselves as threatened by a single, organized protest movement. Most rebellions started over local, isolated issues involving living conditions or specific disciplinary actions, though protests nearly always evolved a common language of defiance against arbitrary authority, particularly in the period of the Revolution. Most disturbances involved little actual rioting or group violence, especially when they were directed against college officials. Typically, they involved fewer than twenty students and lasted no longer than a few hours of a single day or night. Even after the rise of abolition societies, the student uprisings lacked a common ideology and organization. The abolition societies commanded no more than a brief period of concern, and while some of them were indeed suppressed, the most important reasons for their collapse were related to changes in the antislavery movement itself. And when the abolition movement declined in the colleges in the 1840s, the unrest persisted—exactly as it had persisted after the ferment of the Revolution.

Disorder in the personal habits and lives of individual students did become a major preoccupation of college officials. This personal disorder could not be explained merely as a manifestation of eternal boyish roughness or dissipation. The form it took in the early nineteenth century was peculiar to its time. Nor can it be accounted for by a more modern explanation: that it represented only the invention of a new bourgeois imagination that craved order and was captivated by an ideological commitment to self-discipline. According to this view, the perception of disorder in personal life must have been a projection upon an unchanged reality; "disorder" must have been an intellectual construct of minds possessed by a new sensibility. There is simply too much evidence of real disorder to sustain this interpretation. The disorder was novel, and it preceded—and helped to produce—the bourgeois sensibility.

Neither did the perception of disorder and the intolerant sensibility spring simply from the family. It did not result from some change in parental feelings or a new concern for the morals or well-being of sons at college. That concern did exist, and it did find expression, both in books like Edward Hitchcock's and in the correspondence between parents and sons, where even conventional discussions of health and illness assumed an intense degree of concern. One looks in vain, however, for evidence that it was the family that suddenly defined student life as dangerous and demanded a tightening of discipline, a closer supervision over morals and health. The concern over disorder preceded widespread fears of parents for their sons. It resulted from pressures within the colleges themselves.

Disorder, both collective and personal, resulted from changes in the institutional structure of collegiate communities between 1760 and 1860. College officials had inherited traditional ideas about their authority and responsibility, ideas carried forward from the seventeenth and eighteenth centuries. They clung to the old codes of college law, with the same language and assumptions about authority and submission and routine, until well into the nineteenth century. At the same time, they found themselves living in an entirely new institutional environment, without the traditional community that had made the old system function. Much behavior now simply escaped the old institutional controls. When officials tried to assert their ancient authority in a novel setting, they found themselves in conflict with their subjects, both rich and poor. Under the paradoxical conditions of the early nineteenth century, they encountered a rebelliousness attributable to one major cause: the very system of discipline itself.

Paradox and conflict became pervasive qualities of existence in New England colleges. Officials were becoming increasingly intolerant of disorder, especially in personal lives. Faculty minutes and disciplinary records reveal in abundance the sources of greatest irritation everywhere: absences, tardiness, neglect of daily tasks, violations of routine. At the same time, in the presence of a heterogeneous student population containing large numbers of the poor, the lives of students each day and season were becoming less regular, less amenable to old forms of discipline and routine. A massive, grinding resistance to ancient routines had arisen from the necessities of student life in the early nineteenth century.

Not casualness, not some overwrought imagination, but need produced that resistance—the need to work, the need to find food and shelter wherever one could, even if at some distance. Resistance of this kind—almost imperceptible in origin and always ill-understood—had forced the creation of the winter vacation for schoolkeepers; it led to an absurd system of "permissible" inexcusable absences from daily exercises.[36] It was not a case of the poor entering the colleges and smashing them by violence. It was a case of their destroying, merely by their presence, the old institutional arrangements that had enforced order. Disorder came from the mundane realities of student life and from the peculiar institutional weaknesses of the collegiate community in the early nineteenth century.

Notes

1 Hebard to John Hebard, October 25, 1824, Hebard Folder, Amherst College Archives, Amherst, Mass.; W. L. Montague, ed., *Biographical Record of the Alumni of Amherst College, During Its First Half Century, 1821-1871* (Amherst, Mass.: J. E. Williams, 1883), pp. 46-47.

2 Diary of Josiah Cary, March 29, 1827, to August 5, 1828, Cary Folder, Amherst Archives; William G. Hammond, *Remembrance of Amherst: An Undergraduate's Diary, 1846-1848*, ed. George F. Whicher (New York: Columbia University Press, 1946), pp. 22-23, 50, 104-05; Montague, *Biographical Record of Amherst*, pp. 85, 232-33.

3 Diary of Josiah Cary, March 30, 1828, Cary Folder; Farwell to Laura P. Farwell, October 14, 1833, and February 17, 1835, Farwell Folder; "A friend of Good Order" to the faculty, November 26, 1829, Document 69, Amherst College Memorabilia: Faculty Records, 1827-42, all in Amherst Archives.

4 Hebard to John Hebard, May 10, 1825, Hebard Folder; Amherst Faculty Records, April 26, 1832, and December 19, 1832, all in Amherst Archives.

5 William S. Tyler, *History of Amherst College During Its First Half Century, 1821-1871* (Springfield, Mass.: Clark W. Bryan and Company, 1873), pp. 74, 262-63; John Farwell to Laura P. Farwell, April 6, 1833, July 9, 1833, and October 14, 1833, Farwell Folder; Hebard to John Hebard, October 25, 1824, September 30, 1825, and October 23, 1827, Hebard Folder; diary of Josiah Cary, entries after June 4, 1830, Cary Folder, all in Amherst Archives. In 1837 between 100 and 150 Amherst students taught common school in the surrounding countryside, according to one estimate; see Tyler, *Amherst*, p. 263.

6 Montague, *Biographical Record of Amherst*, p. 127; Farwell to Laura P. Farwell, February 16, 1833, and October 14, 1833; Farwell to Stephen Caswell, July 5, 1836, both in Farwell Folder; Hebard to John Hebard, May 7, 1831, Hebard Folder; diary of Josiah Cary, April 6, 1828, Cary Folder, all in Amherst Archives. Farwell's name appears as no. 1698 in the Beneficiary Account Book, American Education Society Archives, Congregational Library, Boston.

7 Farwell to Laura P. Farwell et al., March 7, 1834, Farwell Folder, Amherst Archives.

8 Farwell to Laura P. Farwell, July 6, 1834, and December 14, 1834, Farwell Folder, Amherst Archives.

9 Farwell to Laura P. Farwell, February 17, 1835, Farwell Folder, Amherst Archives.

10 "Records of the Amherst Auxiliary Anti-Slavery Society formed July 19th in Amherst College, 1833-1835," July 19, 1833; "A Copy of the Memorial of the Anti-Slavery Society to the Faculty of Am. College," n.d. (ca. October 13, 1834), in ibid., Amherst Archives. The list of signers actually contains seventy-nine names, four of which are crossed out. Tyler accepted the figure seventy-eight. Beyond the first ten names, it is difficult to determine when individuals signed the constitution. It is likely that most of them signed in the fall of 1834, when faculty opposition to the society prompted a group of students to break into the secretary's room and subscribe their names to the original list. See Tyler, *Amherst*, pp. 246, 249.

11 These statements are based on a comparison of the membership list with Montague's biographical register and the names of beneficiaries in the Beneficiary Account Book, American Education Society Archives. Cf. David Donald, *Lincoln Reconsidered: Essays on the Civil War Era* (New York: Alfred A. Knopf, 1956), pp. 19-36; and Lewis Feuer, *The Conflict of Generations: The Character and Significance of Student Movements* (New York: Basic Books, 1969), pp. 321-23. Feuer denies to American abolitionism the character of a "student movement," excepting only the Lane Rebels of 1833-34. Feuer's argument rests heavily on evidence that makes Lane students appear to have been exceptional; their maturity, Feuer believes, made them "thoroughly atypical of the students in American colleges and universities at the time."

12 Leverett Wilson Spring, *A History of Williams College* (Boston: Houghton Mifflin Company, 1917), pp. 139-40; John King Lord, *A History of Dartmouth College* (Concord, N.H.: Rumford Press, 1913), pp. 249-54; Louis C. Hatch, *The History of Bowdoin College* (Portland, Me.: Loring, Short & Harmon, 1927), pp. 57, 290; Tyler, *Amherst*, p. 249. The second anti-slavery society at Amherst, formed in 1837, declined to correspond as a group with Weld; see "Records of the Amherst College Anti-Slavery Society, 1837-1841," February 7, 1840, Amherst Archives.

13 "Records of the Amherst Auxiliary, 1833-1835," July 24, 1833, February 11, 1834, November 24, 1834, and February 23, 1835; Humphrey to the Committee of the Anti-Slavery Society, November 26, 1834 (copy), "Records of the Amherst Auxiliary, 1833-1835," all in Amherst Archives; Tyler, *Amherst*, pp. 244-50.

14 Farwell to Mrs. Laura Caswell, June 23, 1835, Farwell Folder, Amherst Archives.

15 Tyler, *Amherst*, pp. 250-51.

16 "Records of the Anti-Slavery Society, 1837-1841," passim; Charles M. Atkinson to John M. Tyler, June 12, 1900, Atkinson Folder, all in Amherst Archives.

17 "The Laws of Collegiate Charity Institution in Amherst Massachusetts," n.d. (ca. 1822), Document 1, Amherst College Memorabilia: College Laws, 1825-78, Amherst Archives.

18 Cressy to Thomas Cressy, November 13, 1822, Cressy Folder, Amherst Archives; Francis Wayland and H. L. Wayland, *A Memoir of the Life and Labors of Francis Wayland*, 2 vols. (New York: Sheldon and Company, 1867), 1:205.

19 Hebard to John Hebard, July 23, 1828, Hebard Folder, Amherst Archives.

20 Adams and Hall to the faculty, n.d., Document 94, Amherst College Memorabilia:

Faculty Records, 1827-42, Amherst Archives.

21 Amherst Faculty Records, February 13, 1830, June 23, 1830, July 7, 1830, and March 7, 1832, Amherst Archives.

22 Diary of Josiah Cary, November 22, 1829, Cary Folder; Henry K. Edson to John M. Tyler, June 25, 1900, Edson Folder; D. W. Faunce to John M. Tyler, June 7, 1900, Faunce Folder, all in Amherst Archives.

23 Amherst Faculty Records, October 4, 1825, August [17], 1832, October 10, 1832, February 6, 1833, February 26, 1834, and July 23, 1834, Amherst Archives. The Amherst faculty admonished monitors or acknowledged failures in the monitorial system every year between 1825 and 1832, and at irregular intervals thereafter.

24 Hebard to John Hebard, October 25, 1824, Hebard Folder, Amherst Archives; Julian Sturtevant, *Julian M. Sturtevant: An Autobiography*, ed. J. M. Sturtevant, Jr. (New York: F. H. Revell Company, [1896]), p. 97; Amherst Faculty Records, July 2, 1828, and March 24, 1830, Amherst Archives. On student government, see Documents 1-13, Amherst College Memorabilia: Faculty Records, 1827-42, Amherst Archives; Tyler, *Amherst*, pp. 178-79; and George E. Peterson, *The New England College in the Age of the University* (Amherst, Mass.: Amherst College Press, 1964), pp. 127-28. Peterson places the first experiment much later, in 1883.

25 John Todd, *The Student's Manual*, 3d ed. (Northampton, Mass.: J. H. Butler, 1835), p. 5. The estimate on the number of manuals is based in part on a search of the Evans and Shaw imprint catalogs. It omits a few works that were, in fact, readers or were addressed to young men leaving college. The five manuals that I found comparable to those of the 1830s all appeared after the Revolution. They were as follows: John Mason, *The Student and Pastor* (Exeter, N.H.: Thomas Odiorne, 1794); John Clarke, *Letters to a Student in the University of Cambridge, Massachusetts* (Boston: Samuel Hall, 1796); William Milns, *The Well-Bred Scholar*, 2d ed., rev. and alt. (New York: Literary Printing Office, 1797); Noah Webster, *Letters to a Young Gentleman Commencing His Education* (New Haven: Howe & Spalding, 1823); and Samuel Miller, *Letters on Clerical Manners and Habits: Addressed to a Student in the Theological Seminary at Princeton, N.J.* (New York: G. & C. Carvill, 1827). For a discussion of student manuals, see Charles Homer Haskins, *Studies in Mediaeval Culture* (Oxford, England: Clarendon Press, 1929), pp. 72-91.

26 Todd, *Student's Manual*, p. 5; for passages borrowed by Todd, see ibid., pp. 223-26, and Mason, *Student and Pastor*, chapter 4.

27 [Asa Dodge Smith], *Letters to a Young Student, in the First Stage of a Liberal Education* (Boston: Perkins & Marvin, 1832), pp. 137-74; William Cogswell, *Letters to Young Men Preparing for the Christian Ministry* (Boston: Perkins & Marvin, 1837), pp. 159-71.

28 Todd, *Student's Manual*, pp. 147-49, 247-59; Mason, *Student and Pastor*, p. 43; Clarke, *Letters*, pp. 30-31.

29 Edward Hitchcock, *Dyspepsy Forestalled and Resisted: or Lectures on Diet, Regimen and Employment*, 2d ed. (Amherst, Mass.: J. S. & C. Adams, 1831), pp. 77-78, 152-54, 161-66, 234-67, 353-57; [Smith], *Letters*, p. 166.

30 Tyler, *Amherst*, p. 260; Frederick Rudolph, *Mark Hopkins and the Log* (New Haven: Yale University Press, 1956), p. 122; Carl F. Price, *Wesleyan's First Century* (Middletown, Conn.: Wesleyan University, 1932), p. 81; Amherst faculty, circular letter to parents [1845?], Document 26-1/2, Amherst College Memorabilia: College Laws, 1825-78, Amherst Archives.

31 Amherst Faculty Records, 1830-31, Amherst Archives; minutes of other faculties show the same kind of concerns. Tyler is quoted in Lord, *Dartmouth*, p. 216; for a discussion of discipline, disorder, and a changing sensibility in Europe, see Philippe Aries, *Centuries of Childhood: A Social History of Family Life*, trans. Robert Baldick (New York: Alfred A. Knopf, 1962), pp. 241-68, 315-36.

32 Louis L. Tucker, *Puritan Protagonist: President Thomas Clapp of Yale College* (Chapel Hill: University of North Carolina Press, 1962), pp. 132-43, 232-62; Samuel Eliot Morison, *Three Centuries of Harvard, 1636-1936* (Cambridge, Mass.: Harvard University Press, 1936), pp. 117-18, 133, 162, 211-12; Josiah Quincy, *History of Harvard University*, 2 vols. (Cambridge, Mass.: John Owen, 1840), 2:176-81; Spring, *Williams*, pp. 57-58; Calvin Durfee, *A History of Williams College* (Boston: A. Williams and Company, 1860), pp. 85-86; David A. Wells and S. H. Davis, *Sketches of Williams College* (Williamstown, Mass.: H. S. Taylor, 1847), pp. 19-22; Rudolph, *Mark Hopkins*, p. 119; Walter C. Bronson, *The History of Brown University, 1764-1914* (Providence, R.I.: Brown University, 1914), pp. 116-17, 153.

33 Harvard College, Board of Overseers, *Report of a Committee of the Overseers of Harvard College, January 6, 1825*, no. 3 (Cambridge, Mass.: Harvard University Press—Hilliard and Metcalf, 1825), pp. 42-46; Morison, *Three Centuries*, pp. 208-10,

230-32; Bronson, *Brown*, pp. 185-88; Lord, *Dartmouth*, pp. 276-79; Tyler, *Amherst*, pp. 242-67; Price, *Wesleyan*, p. 65; Hatch, *Bowdoin*, pp. 90-100; Spring, *Williams*, pp. 180-81; Wells and Davis, *Williams*, p. 73; Peterson, *New England College*, pp. 80-148; Julian Ira Lindsay, *Tradition Looks Forward: The University of Vermont; A History, 1791-1904* (Burlington: University of Vermont and State Agricultural College, 1954), p. 150.
34 Sturtevant, *Sturtevant*, pp. 94-95.

35 [Lyman H. Bagg], *Four Years at Yale, By a Graduate of '69* (New Haven: Charles C. Chatfield & Co., 1871), pp. 503-15; *Yale Banner*, November 5, 1841, November 12, 1841; Yale Faculty Records, 1817-51, May 24, 1839, Yale University Archives, New Haven, Conn.; James Clement Moffat to John Sean McCulloch, December 5, 1838, Yale Manuscripts, Misc. S, Yale Archives.
36 Amherst Faculty Records, February 26, 1834, Amherst Archives.

8 In Loco Collegii

The family, with all the sympathies of relationship and society, is the natural place for the young.

Francis Wayland, 1842

Disorder and discipline, timeless concerns of men who have supervised the daily lives of students, bedeviled college faculties in antebellum New England. Disorder became their preoccupation as students scattered into villages to find board, lodging, and work. Discipline problems confounded them as pressures of poverty in the student population fragmented the collegiate community.

The passing of the old residential college and its commons destroyed the institutional setting, which, by the isolation and routine it imposed, had sustained an intimate, "parental" system of government. At one time, faculties had assumed without question the responsibilities of governing scholars *in loco parentis*, but now, suddenly, the obligations became difficult and vexatious. College officers—the president, the professors, the tutors—were losing control over students, whose independence and sociability surpassed all precedents. The reasons were far from timeless; in New England, changes in the demographic and material conditions of student life were generating a crisis in higher education.

More than an old metaphor was lost between 1800 and 1860 when the traditional idea of "parental" government disappeared along with the institutions of collegiate community. The metaphor had represented the only working system of discipline known before the early nineteenth century. It had extended over students in the colonial period an intimate supervision of residence, diet, company, and manners. Teachers assumed the position of parents. Indeed, Harvard laws in 1655 had required students to honor the president, tutors, and fellows "as their Naturall parents." College laws gave no explicit role to a student's family in punishment proceedings; the family relinquished its role, even in serious cases involving a student's separation from the institution. Beginning in 1734, Harvard simply informed parents of fines their sons had incurred in each quarter's term bills. Otherwise, parents learned of difficulties after the issue had been settled. Before the nineteenth century, discipline involved a confrontation between students and officers of the college alone.[1]

This conception of parental government, more rigorous than modern conceptions in its substitution of faculty for family, functioned in a collegiate community designed for familial surveillance. The system included the power to isolate its members in a secluded institution and regulate intimate details of daily life through long periods of a prescribed cycle of study and vacation. Simple principles made it work. The residential college confined young men within observable space for definite periods of time. So long as students could find food, lodging, and work within the college, few would have to leave its grounds and thus escape surveillance. Prayer, recitation, lecture, study, dining, recreation, and sleep followed in orderly, unself-conscious sequences. So long as the annual cycle of study and brief vacations could be maintained—as it largely was through the colonial period—discipline might be imposed *in loco parentis* throughout a student's career.

Erosion began with periodic failures to keep students gathered in the commons and residence halls at Yale and Harvard and with the winter vacation for schoolkeeping. This was in the eighteenth century. In the first half of the nineteenth century, under the impact of infiltration by the poor, the institutional arrangements that had sustained parental discipline simply disappeared. It was the presence of the poor—together with the dissatisfaction of rich students —that destroyed the old seclusion of the college and broke up its ancient routines. It was because of the poor that the commons at all New England colleges closed between 1800 and 1860; a dozen different styles of boarding resulted, all determined by the students themselves. It was the presence of the poor that dispersed the student population, releasing students to the town, removing the possibility of supervising the college intimately and informally in a confined body. It was their presence that caused college laws to become outmoded, for how could one apply to mature men rules and punishments designed for boys? This was the source of the crisis: the colleges of antebellum New England were ill-provided with the means to control student behavior either within their own buildings or in town. Colleges became places that indeed could foster a sensitivity to disorder.

They could also frustrate anyone who was still committed to old obligations and who might try to enforce parental forms of government in a novel institutional setting. Harshness would then replace ease and intimacy; tone would change to preserve substance. Discipline would be reduced to its simplest elements, crime and punishment. Officials would either have to become more punitive—confronting students directly—or they would have to consider governing in some new way.

Problems of controlling students so distracted New England faculties after

1820 that the whole system of parental government came into question. Deliberations about changing the method of discipline began to take place throughout New England, part of a general debate on collegiate education in the antebellum period. The Yale Report of 1828, for all its grand reassertion of the classical curriculum, nevertheless paused to defend the traditional assumptions of "parental superintendence." ("As it is a substitute for the regulations of a family, it should approach as near to the character of parental control as the circumstances of the case will admit.") The Report hinted that "in a large city" an institution might develop along other lines, but it insisted upon the residential college for other locations, certainly for New Haven.

> The parental character of college government, requires that the students should be so collected together, as to constitute one family; that the intercourse between them and their instructors may be frequent and familiar. This renders it necessary that suitable *buildings* be provided, for the residence of the students. . . .[2]

Yale's complacency has obscured the uncertainty at other institutions. Harvard debated its system of government after 1821 with an acrimony that persisted through a pamphlet war and the publication in 1825 of the faculty report on discipline. The Amherst faculty began to consider better ways of controlling students as early as 1825, and it was still looking in 1838 when it initiated a correspondence with other New England colleges on systems of government. Brown revised its system in 1827; Dartmouth appointed a committee to devise "a new mode of college discipline" in 1832, but the committee failed to think of anything new.[3]

Troubles had developed in these institutions that could not be dismissed by invoking stale familial imagery. Not even the Yale faculty was finding that circumstances permitted an easy application of parental superintendence. Its report failed to settle anybody's doubts. Indeed, those doubts became more radical until, in 1842, President Francis Wayland proposed a drastic alternative to the old system. Wayland had tried to tighten discipline at Brown along traditional lines during his fifteen years as president. In his *Thoughts on the Present Collegiate System in the United States,* he confessed that he had failed. His experience had convinced him that parental government had lost its institutional foundation in America and that it ought to be abandoned.[4]

Wayland had discovered the complexities of governing a student population as greatly diversified in age as was New England's. Youngsters of fourteen could enter the same class as young men of twenty-five or thirty, men who had changed their minds about life's chances after some experience in the world. "Here then are students of very dissimilar ages associated together, pursuing the same studies and subjected to the same rules," he observed. "It is obvious that the rules suitable for one party, would be unsuitable for the other; and yet the necessity is apparent of subjecting every member of the same society, to the same regulations." His recent trip to Oxford and Cambridge had drawn his attention to other peculiarities of colleges in New England. They had adopted the English plan of discipline, but their poverty denied them the architectural and residential arrangements to sustain that plan.

English colleges were designed for "the responsibility of moral guard-ianship"; they were built in quadrangles with single gateways attended by por-ters. "If a student is out of his room at night, or if he return to it at a late hour, it is of course known to the officer to whom the student is responsible." Officers lived within the quadrangles and shared common table with students. "In fact, the whole establishment is constructed upon the plan of a common family, all the members inhabiting parts of the same edifice." The plain, spare "colleges" at Brown and Dartmouth and Amherst, designed by poverty itself, offered none of these conveniences or safeguards (see Figure 1). "The build-ings in this country are never constructed with a view to supervision," he said. "They are open from the beginning of the term to the end of it, by day and by night." The college always stood near "the usual temptations of youth," whether in town or in country. "Place it where you will, in a few years, there will cluster around it all the opportunities of idle and vicious expenditure." No walls, no guard at the gate could isolate youth in cheap housing. Moreover, professors commonly married and lived "at a distance from the College premises." Students dined alone; at night junior officers did remain to disperse noisy assemblages and to note whatever absences they could detect during visitation. "They can however do but little more." Under these conditions, students experienced liberation, an immunity against the sanctions of every law. "If we really intend to carry out a system of exact moral re-sponsibility, it is manifest that our arrangements stand in need of a radical change."[5]

When Wayland wrote in 1842, he could not imagine a gathering of fortunes sufficient to construct English colleges all across America. Just to think of magnificent Oxford and Cambridge—"quadrangle after quadrangle"—gave him a "sinking despair" that America would never know "such glorious yet solemn loveliness." Suitable buildings, in the manner prescribed by the Yale Report, could not be built. Wayland proposed to abandon pretention and adopt the model of the Scotch universities. The English model, still idealized in America, provided supervision, residence, and board at great expense. "The Scotch Institutions furnish nothing but Education, and leave the pupil to pro-vide every thing else for himself and are proverbially cheap." Students at Glas-gow and Edinburgh arrived with enough only to subsist and pay tuition. "No one either knows or asks how or where they live." They were assumed to be capable of self-government.

The residential system, having consumed, by Wayland's estimate, $1.5 million for buildings in New England alone, must be scrapped. He suggested that minors might remain with their families while studying. "The family, with all the sympathies of relationship and society, is the natural place for the young." Parents and relatives could impose "restraints" and "inspection" themselves. "The professor must be relieved from much of the police duty which devolves upon him at present." Older students he simply wanted to release. "There is no reason why an instructor should assume any special moral responsibility for young men who have already attained to majority."[6]

Francis Wayland did not intend to liberate students; he did not contemplate a system in which all authority would be suspended. He faulted the college, not for its excessive paternalism, but for the laxness which was releasing youth

FIGURE 1.   Village and college at Amherst, Massachusetts, about 1847. This view from
the southwest shows the college when its buildings and students still related closely to the
village and its society. Later, the college would turn its front away from the town, creating
an inner campus with new buildings behind these, grouped in a rectangle. The original
buildings, built in the plain style of the early nineteenth century, now form the west wall of
the rectangle. (From the college catalog of 1847-48, courtesy of Amherst College Archives.)

from the very discipline that its buildings were supposed to impose. Intended
agents of discipline were actually freeing youth, and Wayland—representing
a continuity with old feelings—could not see how those agents might ever
be used to restore order. When he began to consider the family as a check
upon students, however, he advanced a major innovation.

Between 1820 and 1840, college officials throughout New England began
to sense, with Wayland, the futility of trying to control students according
to traditional, but increasingly rigid, procedures. To have insisted upon parental
powers, to have tightened detection and hardened punishment would have
transformed the New England college into an altogether different institution.
Albert Hopkins at Williams knew this. "Whatever may be the theory of some,
wiser than ourselves," he said, "we hope the day may be far distant, when
this College shall come to be regarded as a house of correction."[7] Since no

TABLE 9   Revivals at Five New England Colleges, 1741-1840

	1741-1800	1801-10	1811-20	1821-30	1831-40	Total
Yale	3	2	3	7	4	19
Dartmouth	4	0	2	2	1	9
Williams	0	1	2	3	4	10
Middlebury		2	3	2	3	10
Amherst				3	2	5
Total	7	5	10	17	14	53

Sources: Henry Wood, "Historical Sketch of the Revivals of Religion in Dartmouth College, Hanover, N.H.," *American Quarterly Register*, 9 (1836): 177-82; [Chauncey] Goodrich, "Narrative of Revivals of Religion in Yale College," ibid., 10 (1838): 289-310; Heman Humphrey, "Revivals of Religion in Amherst College," ibid., 11 (1839): 317-28; Joshua Bates, "Revivals of Religion in Middlebury College," ibid., 12 (1840): 305-23; Albert Hopkins, "Revivals of Religion in Williams College," ibid., 13 (1841): 341-51, 461-74.

one had anticipated the institutional consequences of social change in the student population, alternative ways of ordering life were slow to be devised.

Piety became one way of thinking about order. In the mind of the elder President Dwight at Yale, religion became "the regulation of our desires, the government of our passions." To lay a check upon evils in literary institutions, Albert Hopkins declared that "nothing is adequate but the power and sanctions of a spiritual religion." For these men, whose language of religion expressed their desire for discipline, revivals assumed a peculiar importance. Of all the measures known in the early nineteenth century for promoting an inner self-discipline, by far the greatest hopes were placed upon the religious revival. Revivals quickened among New England students after 1800, as they did among the general populace (see Table 9). Yale experienced perhaps as few as three revivals between 1741 and 1800; between 1801 and 1840, it was visited sixteen or seventeen times, an average of nearly one revival every two years. They occurred frequently elsewhere, too.[8]

Clearly, the college revivals accompanied the Second Great Awakening and were not peculiar to the student population. Contemporary narratives indicate that revivals in towns sometimes ignited the colleges, sometimes not. Still, conditions peculiar to the colleges were at work among students. College officials promoted revivals for the acknowledged purpose of improving discipline. They sought revivals to save souls, but they valued them frankly for the sake of order. If the revivals that swept through northern colleges after 1800 can be considered in terms of a social movement, it is only as a movement impelled by leaders of the education societies and faculties. Faculty members, not students, were nearly always the active agents. Only rarely did pious students take the lead, as in the Williams revival of 1806. Indeed, faculties occasionally admonished beneficiaries and members of student religious societies for failing to display the piety that might prompt a revival. At the same time, officials discouraged students from promoting revivals outside the colleges. Had this been a student movement, it would have been suppressed, as the first Yale awakening and the antislavery movements were suppressed.[9]

In describing these events, narratives of the collegiate revivals employed a single, universal concept of moral transformation. "The whole aspect of College was immediately changed," wrote Story Hebard of the revival in 1831 at Amherst. "Many of the most thoughtless & Immoral young men here, have submitted themselves to Jesus Christ & are now singing the songs of Redeeming love."[10] When the American Education Society began to gather accounts of collegiate revivals in the late 1830s, the narratives exhibited some striking similarities. All followed the conventional form of the revival narrative, speculating as to causes, discussing numbers converted, and describing opponents. And while popular convention also required some treatment of moral transformation in the community or congregation, in the college narratives this became the central concern. In this forum, the revival was primarily a regulating agent: the new piety was "an aid to discipline and government in institutions of learning." Moral evils had always prevailed before each revival, and college government had always been maintained "with difficulty."[11] Before the Williams revival of 1812, Albert Hopkins reported, "it became a trial to live in college, especially in the building occupied by the two lower classes." Then came a revival, and with revival came change.

> The results were permanent. Those various petty mischiefs and tricks which had been so common before, entirely disappeared, and during the three years which followed, the students pursued their appropriate pursuits, in an atmosphere quiet and tranquil, congenial to mental improvement as well as growth in divine things.[12]

Until the 1830s, college revivals appear to have been conducted like revivals in any ordinary community, with the same measures employed and with no distinctions drawn between churches and colleges. All the narratives list similar revival techniques: visits from room to room, prayer meetings in the evening, preaching at both regular and special services, followed—after 1829—by an occasional protracted meeting. By 1840, college officials had sensed danger in some methods, as, indeed, had many ministers; revivals might promote discord, as President Clap had feared. The reports themselves reveal the kind of disorders such events could produce. They might excite animal feelings and derange the whole routine of collegiate institutions. "There is apt to be a strong disposition to multiply meetings too much, and to depend upon them, to the neglect of prayer," warned Heman Humphrey. "This I have witnessed more than once. There is danger, also, of visiting and talking too much, especially in the height of a revival, and when many are borne down with distress." President Joshua Bates of Middlebury called for principles of more "prudent management." Everyone now agreed that academic exercises must not be interrupted during revivals. The problem lay in devising measures to avoid disrupting the colleges while promoting what Albert Hopkins termed "a more permanent religious order."[13]

Hopkins's narrative of revivals at Williams, the last in the series published by the American Education Society, depicted the new measures designed to advance that order. Hopkins had invented the "noon meeting" for prayer in 1832, a "dam at midday" to prevent religious feeling "from being overflown, and everything relapsing, again, into a stagnant and dead state, as had been the case after most previous revivals." Sometimes as many as seventy students met at noon, about half the enrollment. "It has served as a balance wheel, to check the irregular movements of individual action, to temper well-meaning, but injudicious zeal." Friday evening "class meetings" began sometime between 1827 and 1831, when, on one occasion at least, students were moved to public confession. "Among those things which weighed most heavily, were neglect and abuse of the Sabbath and the Bible, lying to officers of college, stealing, card playing, drinking, keeping liquor at their rooms." The possibilities fascinated Hopkins. "Their confessions, as might be supposed, were cruel darts to the companions of those who had made them, who now stood revealed, as guilty of the same things," he said. "There began to be a glimpse of what is implied in a pure community, and a hope that such a condition was about to be realized by us." Hopkins announced the achievement of that community, the establishment of a permanent religious order at Williams, in the decade after the revival of 1831. There had been "a general improvement in the order of College, petty annoyances have become less frequent, [while] cases of discipline have been rare."[14]

Men like Albert Hopkins, who tried to discipline college life through revivals of religion, actually were extending to students a form of adult, non-academic discipline. Half consciously, they had abandoned the tone of parental government in favor of fraternal solicitude, yet they knew that as an instrument of discipline in colleges the revival had certain flaws. In crucial ways, a student community could not function like an ordinary community. Colleges were inherently less stable than churches, for example; the effects of revivals were muted by vacations, and they were less enduring because of the inevitable turnover of succeeding classes. Maintaining religious emotion at fever pitch among each successive class was strenuous work for the faculty. And as Hopkins himself confessed, revivals alone had not brought order to Williams. Though they continued to occur in New England into the last half of the nineteenth century, collegiate revivals ultimately gave way to forms of discipline that worked in very different ways.

In time, the colleges followed neither the recommendations of the Yale Report nor those of Francis Wayland; they neither reasserted their parental duties nor surrendered all governance. Even though the choice was posed in mutually exclusive terms, they chose not to take either of these alternatives; they did not borrow from England or from Scotland. In disconnected fashion, without plan or articulation and through hundreds of separate decisions, the faculties in New England devised an original alternative. They addressed themselves to concrete problems: vacations, monitors, prizes, ranking, the merit roll, attendance, punishment, excuses, recordkeeping, the allocation of duties. Mundane matters, sometimes written down in question-and-answer form, burdened the documents of their deliberations, denying them the grandeur of the Yale Report or the coherence of Wayland's *Thoughts*. Yet here, slowly, cumulatively, a transformation of great magnitude began to take place. Hereafter, order would be imposed through a student's daily academic performance—and discipline through the influence of his own family. Scholarship would become a competitive activity and discipline an internalized matter of self-control and family watchfulness. The intellectual life of the student was transformed, and the modern system of discipline was born.

Modern terminology still employs the phrase *in loco parentis* to describe collegiate government in the twentieth century, though historically it is more accurate to recognize that certain roles have been reversed and that, after the early nineteenth century, the family began to perform disciplinary functions, *in loco collegii*. College officials ceased to act in place of parents, at least by standards of the eighteenth century. They no longer spanked or fined; they rarely administered punishments directly, preferring simply to dismiss or degrade. They quietly discarded the old system and never resurrected it in pure form. By 1871, Lyman Bagg (Yale, 1869) could reveal the change to prospective Yale students.

> Where a man is, or what he is doing, outside the hours when his presence is required at recitation, lecture, or chapel, the faculty make no effort to enquire. The "paternal" theory of government is not much insisted upon by them.[15]

Rather, the faculty implicated parents more directly in the process of discipline, and at earlier stages. By 1833, Amherst voted to warn parents when sons merely risked punishment for absences.[16] Parents would punish; parents would be compelled to assume responsibility for the behavior of sons at school. Francis Wayland had begun this transfer of authority in his reforms of 1827 at Brown: "The parent was the individual with whom all intercourse respecting the son was carried on, whereas, hitherto, the dealing had been mainly with the pupil himself."[17] The family had not intruded itself into areas once the province of others. New sentiments concerning the nature of childhood and the raising of children, as well as new convictions about family prerogatives, did not cause parents to demand these duties for themselves. Colleges had sought the aid of the family; faculties had invoked that aid, insisting that the dangers of college life demanded it.

The invention of the grading system at New England colleges after 1825 provided the crucial means for shifting responsibilities to the family. Once faculties had devised grading, they could merely presume to judge academic performance, while they handed major problems of punishment to the family. Primitive ranking schemes appeared in the eighteenth century at Harvard and Yale, though nearly a century passed before a clear conception emerged that scholarship itself was being judged. Harvard appears to have taken academic performance into account in its placing system for a brief period early in the eighteenth century. Yale developed an idea of grading very slowly after 1783, when President Stiles began to rank scholars in four groups—*optimi*, second *optimi, inferiores (boni)*, and *pejores*. In 1813 Yale began to keep a record book with a numerical scale to grade student examinations twice each year. None of these schemes appears to have been associated with discipline, however.[18]

Grading established itself in its modern function after 1825, when the Harvard Overseers published a description of their new system. The Overseers had voted to abolish fines, an important instrument of the old system, forcing themselves to cast about for some substitute. Even as they reasserted the "parental" nature of government at Harvard, they began to involve the family in discipline through grading.

> Every quarter bill of each Student is to be accompanied by a statement, from the Records, of every mark of approbation or distinction he has received in the quarter, and of every punishment or censure he has incurred, of all his absences from exercises, lectures, and publick worship, and his merit as a scholar, with any other information, which in the opinion of the Government will be useful to the parents; and a copy of the quarter bill and of this statement is to be sent to the parent or guardian.[19]

Comparable merit systems appeared at once in other institutions. Amherst adopted a "scale of merit in recitation" in October 1825 and devised forms for keeping records on scholarship and absence by 1828. Brown, Vermont, and Bowdoin adopted marking systems by 1827, Dartmouth by 1828. Each of these plans had its own peculiarities, suggesting that they may have been invented in isolation. Officials may not have consulted one another directly until 1838, when the Amherst faculty began to compile a study of procedures at other institutions.[20]

Certain common practices were emerging. By 1838, precise records of academic work were being kept each day at Amherst, Bowdoin, Harvard, Yale, and Dartmouth; Yale and Dartmouth assigned grades "at the moment of reciting." Numerical judgments of "general deportment" and "application to study"—as distinct from scholarship itself—also went into these records, along with marks for absences.[21] Between 1850 and 1875, students would also begin to be graded on written examinations.[22] These marks then were used to determine a student's rank on merit rolls. Instructors made the computations; no longer would students vote—as those at Yale had done until 1830—"respecting the relative rank of their fellows."[23] This would be determined from records comparable in many ways to the schedules devised by the American Education Society.

Yet, as late as the 1830s, college officials still had not determined exactly how to use the merit roll. According to earlier practice, faculties had communicated the results of examinations directly to the students, a custom that evidently failed to induce sufficient zeal. To whom should all these computations be revealed? Dartmouth, perhaps in confusion, sent its first merit reports to the trustees.[24] Harvard alone sent regular reports to parents in the 1820s, though Amherst and Brown would send reports at the parent's request. As late as 1838, the Amherst faculty found that Yale, Dartmouth, Vermont, and Middlebury sent no regular reports to parents; it appeared that Vermont had no merit system at all. When colleges did report to parents, their emphasis fell heavily on absences and deportment. "No College reports scholarship," the Amherst survey discovered. The labors of recordkeeping argued against it, but the merit roll would become a powerful instrument of discipline only when officials used it to involve the family. Amherst at last adopted a system of regular parental reports, including grades for scholarship, in 1838.[25] Its reports made scholarship more central to discipline than those devised by Harvard in 1825 and soon were adopted everywhere.

Grading, marking, the merit roll, parental reports—these reforms were introduced as disciplinary procedures, never purely as a means to elevate the standards of scholarship in New England. Scholarship may have improved as a consequence of these reforms, but neither grading nor reporting was undertaken for that motive. Grading evolved in association with discipline; a student's poor academic performance was nearly always cited to support some other grounds for censure. Rarely was an antebellum student dismissed from college for poor scholarship alone, though it now had become possible to fail and perhaps be denied a degree because of bad marks.

Discipline that was more constant, more certain than "parental government" by professors had come into existence with grading and scholastic reports which were sent to the family. The task of achieving some standard of performance each day would exact a routine of its own kind to replace institutional routines of the old collegiate community. The resultant family watchfulness, together with a new sense of competition among classmates, improved upon the supervision of college officials. Discipline ceased to be a source of direct conflict between students and faculty as many of its functions were removed from the college and returned to the family.

By 1900, the student population had been brought to order. After the Civil War, through a massive and expensive effort to revive the residential college—to recreate what had become a romantic conception of the collegiate community—students again began to gather for meals and lodging within institutions striving to imitate old forms. The universities at New Haven and Cambridge succeeded best in constructing buildings that expressed a desire to recreate the intimacy and shelter of the traditional English college. A new prosperity, beyond the range of Francis Wayland's antebellum imagination, also permitted New England colleges to reinvent scholarships for the poor on a scale unprecedented for America. This meant that, for the first time since the eighteenth century, college officials could control charitable funds and the selection of beneficiaries. At the same time, they enhanced their power to select the entire student population. They could now afford to come to terms with the demographic changes of the early nineteenth century by selecting students who were younger, more uniform in their ages, more affluent and homogeneous in their social origins, and—to complement the new system of discipline—more dependent upon their families. The laggards, the independent poor, the destroyers of community, these would lose their influence.

To have accepted the conditions of student life as it had existed in antebellum New England, college officials must necessarily have been willing to accept institutional changes as fundamental as any introduced by the rise of universities in America after 1860. In order to accommodate the independent poor—especially without the backing of large scholarship funds—they would have had to put aside both the notion of an uninterrupted, four-year course in residence and their preoccupation with constant attendance and performance in the classroom. They must have been willing to surrender the orderliness of predictable routines and a predictable source of revenue from unvarying numbers of students with assured amounts of tuition money to pay. They must have been willing to permit the destruction of the entire institutional setting for higher education.

The transformation of student life in New England did not proceed to its ultimate, logical consequence—a chaos of institutional collapse. Even before the Civil War, a new order began to evolve in the student population through the workings of the new system of discipline. After 1865, this order was advanced through a counterreformation of institutions modeled on memories of the ancient, venerable collegiate community.

Still, changes in the early nineteenth century left a lasting impression on student life and higher education. The new discipline was itself a product of antebellum change which survived into the twentieth century, one of several legacies to modernity from the period of paupers and scholars. And the pre-Civil War style of living, with its expanded personal options and liberties, continued to characterize student society after 1860, since the residential college never regained its powers to seclude and supervise. Some students continued to escape the residential college, and, until 1900 at least, they enjoyed the independence acquired by students in the preceding hundred years. Within the colleges, the social classes maintained the physical separation that had appeared in the 1820s. These were inheritances that survived long past 1860.

Although New England's student population did expand significantly between 1800 and 1860, the numerical increase was absorbed more by the founding of new colleges than by the growth of older ones. This meant that the reshaping of the region's collegiate life in this period occurred at a time when—long before institutions on the scale of the great modern universities were even imagined—American colleges were still very small. (As late as 1859-60, for example, only five hundred undergraduates were enrolled at Yale, the largest school of its kind.) Thus, whatever changes took place in student life in these years were not the result of dramatic institutional growth: indeed, the very smallness of the colleges and the meagerness of their means made them all the more susceptible to change. The transformation of college society really began in the villages and farming communities of New England, when hundreds of impecunious young men made up their minds to become scholars at the little colleges in Williamstown, Middlebury, and Hanover. Their presence in those schools resulted in a social diversity that was far more significant than any mere increase in the number of enrolled students, representing as it did the social forces that were reforging New England society.

Notes

1 "The Lawes of the Colledge published publiquely before the Students of Harvard Colledge May 4. 1655," in Samuel Eliot Morison, ed., *Harvard College Records*, Publications of the Colonial Society of Massachusetts (Boston, 1935), 3:329-30. This injunction appeared in similar language in the laws of 1734, but it was altered in those of 1767, when the familial analogy disappeared. See also Josiah Quincy, *History of Harvard University*, 2 vols. (Cambridge, Mass.: John Owen, 1840), 1:389, 393.

2 "Original Papers in relation to a Course of Liberal Education," *American Journal of Science and Arts* 15 (1829): 303.

3 Samuel Eliot Morison, *Three Centuries of Harvard, 1636-1936* (Cambridge, Mass.: Harvard University Press, 1936), pp. 230-

33; George S. Hilliard et al., *Life, Letters, and Journals of George Ticknor*, 2 vols. (Boston: James R. Osgood and Company, 1876), 1:354-60; Harvard College, Board of Overseers, *Report of a Committee of the Overseers of Harvard College, January 6, 1825*, no. 3 (Cambridge, Mass.: University Press—Hilliard and Metcalf, 1825), passim; Amherst Faculty Records, September 26, 1825, October 4, 1825, June 26, 1828, July 22, 1835, October 25, 1837, and October 26, 1838, Amherst College Archives, Amherst, Mass.; Report of a committee, July 25, 1838, Document 161, Amherst College Memorabilia: Faculty Records, 1827-42, Amherst Archives; Francis Wayland and H. L. Wayland, *A Memoir of the Life and Labors of Francis Wayland*, 2 vols. (New York: Sheldon and Company, 1867), 1:204-09; John King Lord, *A History of Dartmouth College* (Concord, N.H.: Rumford Press, 1913), p. 277.

4 Francis Wayland, *Thoughts on the Present Collegiate System in the United States* (Boston: Gould, Kendall & Lincoln, 1842), pp. 130-31; see also Theodore R. Crane, "Francis Wayland and the Residential College," *Rhode Island History* 29 (1960): 65-78, 118-28.

5 Wayland, *Thoughts*, pp. 29-31, 119-23.

6 Ibid., pp. 116-17, 126-29, 144-45.

7 Albert Hopkins, "Revivals of Religion in Williams College," *American Quarterly Register* 13 (1841): 474.

8 These figures on revivals are based on the following narratives: Henry Wood, "Historical Sketch of the Revivals of Religion in Dartmouth College, Hanover, N.H.," *American Quarterly Register* 9 (1836): 177-82; [Chauncey A.] Goodrich, "Narrative of Revivals of Religion in Yale College," *American Quarterly Register* 10 (1838): 289-310; Heman Humphrey, "Revivals of Religion in Amherst College," *American Quarterly Register* 11 (1839): 317-28; Joshua Bates, "Revivals of Religion in Middlebury College," *American Quarterly Register* 12 (1840): 305-23; Albert Hopkins, "Revivals of Religion in Williams College," *American Quarterly Register* 13 (1841): 341-51, 461-74.

9 Hopkins, "Revivals in Williams," pp. 345-47; "Constitution and Records of the Monthly Concert of Prayer, 1829-1842," American Education Society Records, November 8, 1831, July 3, 1832, and December 5, 1837, Amherst Archives; Amherst Faculty Records, October 31, 1825, November 4, 1825, and April 27, 1836, Amherst Archives.

10 Hebard to John Hebard, May 7, 1831, Hebard Folder, Amherst Archives.

11 Wood, "Revivals in Dartmouth," p. 182; Hopkins, "Revivals in Williams," p. 344.

12 Hopkins, "Revivals in Williams," pp. 348-51.

13 Humphrey, "Revivals in Amherst," pp. 319-23, 327-28; Bates, "Revivals in Middlebury," pp. 313, 319-21; Hopkins, "Revivals in Williams," p. 467; Goodrich, "Revivals in Yale," pp. 302-08.

14 Hopkins, "Revivals in Williams," pp. 467-71.

15 [Lyman H. Bagg], *Four Years at Yale, By a Graduate of '69* (New Haven: Charles C. Chatfield & Co., 1871), p. 588.

16 Amherst Faculty Records, February 28, 1833, Amherst Archives.

17 Wayland and Wayland, *Memoir of Wayland*, 1:205-06.

18 Mary L. Smallwood, *An Historical Study of Examinations and Grading Systems in Early American Universities* (Cambridge, Mass.: Harvard University Press, 1935), pp. 42-47; Morison, *Three Centuries*, pp. 104-05; Book of Averages, "Record of Examinations," 1813-39, Yale University Archives, New Haven, Conn.

19 Harvard, *Report of the Overseers*, pp. vii-ix.

20 Most of the evidence for these statements on the origins of marking and reporting comes from the manuscript faculty minutes and records of Amherst, Harvard, Yale, Bowdoin, Vermont, and Middlebury. These records are deposited in the archives or special collections of each institution. See also Amherst Faculty Records, October 4, 1825, Amherst Archives; Wayland and Wayland, *Memoir of Wayland*, 1:205; Louis C. Hatch, *The History of Bowdoin College* (Portland, Me.: Loring, Short & Harmon, 1927), pp. 236-37; Lord, *Dartmouth*, pp. 213-14; and Ernest C. Marriner, *The History of Colby College* (Waterville, Me.: Colby College Press, 1963), p. 100.

21 Report, Document 161, Amherst Faculty Records, 1827-42, Amherst Archives.

22 Francis Wayland urged the adoption of written examinations as early as 1842; see Wayland, *Thoughts*, pp. 99-101.

23 Noah Porter, "Additional Notices," in *Yale College, a Sketch of Its History*, ed. William L. Kingsley, 2 vols. (New York: Henry Holt and Company, 1879), 2:504-05.

24 Lord, *Dartmouth*, p. 213.

25 Report, Document 161, Amherst Faculty Records, 1827-42, Amherst Archives; report of the committee on merit roll, n.d. (ca. 1838), Document 172, ibid.

APPENDIXES

Appendix A

The Ages of
New England Students

As the student population of New England grew, so did the number of mature students (see Table 1). Between the Revolution and the Civil War, mature students—who graduated at twenty-five or older—became a large group within this population, sizable enough to change the character of the colleges.[1] A census of any decade between 1800 and 1860 would reveal that the mature students gathered primarily at the provincial colleges, particularly at those drawing students from the hill country of western and northern New England. Harvard and Yale shared some of the influx of older men, but to a lesser degree than the new colleges (see Tables 11 and 12).

Age distribution at Harvard and Yale differed significantly from that at the new colleges in most decades. Generally, the age curves for Harvard and Yale between 1761 and 1860 peaked sharply at ages twenty to twenty-two. Curves for the new colleges were rounded, rather than peaked, and were high on the side of maturity (see Graphs 1-3). A peaked curve for nineteenth-century graduates is a sign that the average student's college career differed little from those of his classmates; a graph of this type suggests that the great majority of students started school early, proceeded without interruption, and came from relatively similar social backgrounds. In contrast, a rounded curve is the sure sign of varied student careers, poverty, and heterogeneous social origins.

The student population in the late colonial period still displayed a uniformly youthful age structure (see Table 10 and Graph 1). By the early nineteenth century, the influx of mature young men had begun. Both Yale and Harvard experienced the early stages of this movement between 1771 and 1800 (see Table 1 and Graph 4). By 1800, the influx was most apparent at the well-established new colleges—Dartmouth, Brown, and Williams—which were receiving students from the Connecticut River Valley and the hill towns of Worcester County, western Massachusetts, and upper New England (see Table 11). Between 1810 and 1860 the mature flooded into all the provincial colleges and gathered in significant numbers and percentages even at Yale (see Table 12 and Graph 4). Harvard experienced a long decline in its portion of mature students between 1800 and 1880, a trend at odds with that at Yale and the provincial colleges. Harvard differed because it drew heavily from the Boston area (where college preparation was easily available to younger students); because it possessed comparatively greater financial-aid funds for poor students (who did continue to enroll); and because it early became the institution of a wealthy, social elite.

Generally, the great period of maturity in the student population occurred between 1801 and 1860. The mature were poor students whose college careers had been delayed. The association of maturity with poverty was evident in the first twenty-one classes at Amherst College, for example. Beneficiaries of the American Education Society formed a disproportionate number of older graduates, and seldom did graduates younger than twenty-two or twenty-three appear on A.E.S. charity lists (see Table 13).

By the early twentieth century, the precocious young graduates of twenty years or younger had almost disappeared as secondary schooling established more uniform stages of college preparation in America. The number of laggards remained fairly constant through 1900, in part because Harvard and Yale began to admit mature students to new university programs. The percentage of laggards in the student population began to decline sharply, however, returning to a level close to that of 150 years earlier (see Table 1 and Graph 4). By 1900, the age curves for almost every New England college had assumed a sharp, peaked appearance like that of Harvard for 1851-60, with modes at twenty-two or twenty-three. The modern homogeneity of age structure in each college class had made its appearance everywhere.[2]

Notes

1   Most studies of European universities use the age at matriculation to determine the relative maturity of student populations. For New England, the evidence does not consistently record age at admission; it is possible to deal uniformly with students at all institutions more simply by using the age at graduation. This method creates no bias toward maturity. In New England, almost all students graduated with the class they originally joined. Regardless of how often they might have left school to work, few of them dropped back to a later graduating class. Delays in completing education nearly always came before, not during, college. This method actually reduces one source of possible bias toward maturity that was inherent in the age at matriculation in New England, where some students (like Mark Hopkins) began their collegiate careers with "advanced standing" in the sophomore or junior classes. Generally, however, the rule was an uninterrupted course of four years, regardless of absences.

2   See W. Scott Thomas, "Changes in the Age of College Graduation," *Popular Science Monthly*, 63 (1903): 159-71.

TABLE 10 Ages of Graduates, 1751-60

	Harvard		Yale		Total	
	No.	%	No.	%	No.	%
18*	44	16.2	34	12.5	78	14.3
19	62	22.8	32	11.8	94	17.3
20	62	22.8	60	22.1	122	22.4
21	41	15.1	52	19.1	93	17.1
22	22	8.1	25	9.2	47	8.6
23	14	5.1	20	7.4	34	6.3
24	7	2.6	22	8.1	29	5.3
25	8	2.9	11	4.0	19	3.5
26	3	1.1	6	2.2	9	1.7
27	5	1.8	4	1.5	9	1.7
28*	4	1.5	6	2.2	10	1.8
Known	272		272		544	
Unknown	1		18		19	
TOTAL	273		290		563	
25 & Older	20	7.4	27	9.9	47	8.6

Sources: Clifford K. Shipton, *Sibley's Harvard Graduates*, vols. 13 and 14 (Boston: Massachusetts Historical Society, 1965 and 1968); and Franklin B. Dexter, *Biographical Sketches of the Graduates of Yale College*, vol. 2 (New York: Henry Holt and Company, 1896).

Note: Percentages are based on the number of known ages; percentages may not add because of rounding.

*These ages include graduates younger than 18 and older than 28.

TABLE 11   Ages of Graduates, 1801-10

| | Amherst | | Bowdoin | | Brown | | Dartmouth | | Middle. | | Vermont | |
	No.	%	No.	%	No.	%	No.	%	No.	%	No.	%
18*			4	11.4	24	12.1	17	5.1	7	8.3	3	15.8
19			11	31.4	14	7.1	18	5.4	5	6.0	1	5.3
20			6	17.1	27	13.6	31	9.4	5	6.0	4	21.1
21			6	17.1	28	14.1	40	12.1	7	8.3	2	10.5
22			4	11.4	30	15.2	42	12.7	10	11.9	4	21.1
23			2	5.7	19	9.6	40	12.1	11	13.1	2	10.5
24			0	0.0	18	9.1	31	9.4	13	15.5	0	0.0
25			0	0.0	16	8.1	34	10.3	15	17.9	1	5.3
26			0	0.0	9	4.5	26	7.9	2	2.4	1	5.3
27			0	0.0	6	3.0	21	6.3	2	2.4	1	5.3
28*			2	5.7	7	3.5	31	9.4	7	8.3	0	0.0
Known			35		198		331		84		19	
?			0		59		6		9		28	
TOTAL			35		257		337		93		47	
25+			2	5.7	38	19.1	112	33.8	26	31.0	3	15.8

Sources: Biographical registers and faculty records.

Note: Percentages are based on the number of known ages; percentages may not add because of rounding.

*These ages include graduates younger than 18 and older than 28.

TABLE 11—Continued

Waterv.		Williams		Harvard		Yale		New Coll.		Ten Coll.	
No.	%	No.	%	No.	%	No.	%	No.	%	No.	%
		16	7.5	39	9.0	69	13.5	71	8.1	179	9.8
		19	9.0	79	18.2	83	16.2	68	7.7	230	12.6
		31	14.6	85	19.6	86	16.8	104	11.8	275	15.1
		33	15.6	66	15.2	78	15.2	116	13.2	260	14.2
		21	9.9	43	9.9	56	10.9	111	12.6	210	11.5
		16	7.5	38	8.8	50	9.7	90	10.2	178	9.8
		27	12.7	29	6.7	40	7.8	89	10.1	158	8.7
		16	7.5	16	3.7	22	4.3	82	9.3	120	6.6
		8	3.8	9	2.1	11	2.1	46	5.2	66	3.6
		11	5.2	12	2.8	11	2.1	41	4.7	64	3.5
		14	6.6	17	3.9	7	1.4	61	6.9	85	4.7
		212		433		513		879		1,825	
		18		32		27		120		179	
		230		465		540		999		2,004	
		49	23.1	54	12.5	51	9.9	230	26.2	335	18.4

TABLE 12   Ages of Graduates, 1851-60

	Amherst		Bowdoin		Brown		Dartmouth		Middle.		Vermont	
	No.	%	No.	%	No.	%	No.	%	No.	%	No.	%
18*	1	0.2	1	0.3	5	1.7	5	0.8	0	0.0	1	0.6
19	8	1.7	16	4.4	11	3.6	11	1.7	3	2.2	3	1.8
20	24	5.2	55	15.3	34	11.2	35	5.4	9	6.7	21	12.7
21	61	13.2	55	15.3	59	19.5	83	12.7	16	11.9	27	16.3
22	61	13.2	47	13.1	47	15.5	96	14.7	23	17.2	29	17.5
23	57	12.3	46	12.8	40	13.2	81	12.4	14	10.4	15	9.0
24	53	11.4	43	11.9	34	11.2	93	14.3	22	16.4	19	11.4
25	47	10.2	40	11.1	23	7.6	80	12.3	9	6.7	18	10.8
26	57	12.3	18	5.0	15	5.0	51	7.8	15	11.2	17	10.2
27	41	8.9	15	4.2	16	5.3	50	7.7	12	9.0	6	3.6
28*	53	11.4	24	6.7	19	6.3	67	10.3	11	8.2	10	6.0
Known	463		360		303		652		134		166	
?	0		0		27		3		0		34	
TOTAL	463		360		330		655		134		200	
25+	198	42.8	97	26.9	73	24.1	248	38.0	47	35.1	51	30.7

Sources: Biographical registers and faculty records.

Note: Percentages are based on the number of known ages; percentages may not add because of rounding.

*These ages include graduates younger than 18 and older than 28.

TABLE 12—Continued

| Waterv. | | Williams | | Harvard | | Yale | | New Coll. | | Ten Coll. | |
No.	%	No.	%	No.	%	No.	%	No.	%	No.	%
0	0.0	4	0.9	2	0.2	3	0.3	17	0.6	22	0.5
1	0.8	15	3.3	41	4.9	39	3.9	68	2.6	148	3.3
5	4.2	56	12.2	172	20.6	109	10.9	239	9.0	520	11.6
12	10.2	84	18.3	262	31.4	243	24.2	397	14.9	902	20.1
14	11.9	73	15.9	194	23.3	211	21.0	390	14.7	795	17.7
14	11.9	64	13.9	81	9.7	129	12.9	331	12.5	541	12.0
14	11.9	51	11.1	35	4.2	97	9.7	329	12.4	461	10.3
23	19.5	38	8.3	21	2.5	60	6.0	278	10.5	359	8.0
11	9.3	30	6.5	12	1.4	39	3.9	214	8.1	265	5.9
7	5.9	18	3.9	5	0.6	30	3.0	165	6.2	200	4.5
17	14.4	27	5.9	9	1.1	43	4.3	228	8.6	280	6.2
118		460		834		1,003		2,656		4,493	
6		21		37		2		91		130	
124		481		871		1,005		2,747		4,623	
58	49.2	113	24.6	47	5.6	172	17.1	885	33.3	1,104	24.6

TABLE 13   Ages of Amherst College Graduates, 1822-42

	?	18*	19	20	21	22	23	24	25	26	27	28	29	30†	Known Ages	Mean Ages	Median Ages
Beneficiaries	2	1	4	7	5	8	12	26	28	26	30	31	15	18	211	25.8	26
Others	11	21	42	77	54	59	53	43	46	42	25	16	15	12	505	22.9	22
Total	13	22	46	84	59	67	65	69	74	68	55	47	30	30	716	23.8	24

Sources: W. L. Montague, ed., *Biographical Record of the Alumni of Amherst College, During Its First Half Century, 1821-1871* (Amherst, Mass.: J. E. Williams, 1883), pp. 9-194; Beneficiary Account Book, American Education Society Archives, Congregational Library, Boston, Mass.

Note: Figures for beneficiaries include only those graduates whose names appeared on charity lists of the American Education Society.

*These figures include graduates younger than 18.
†These figures include graduates older than 30.

GRAPH 1   Age Distribution of Harvard and Yale Graduates, 1751-60

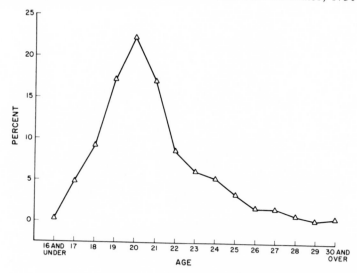

GRAPH 2   Age Distribution of New England Graduates, 1801-10

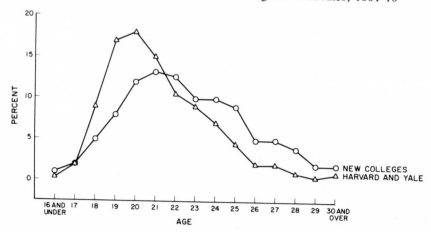

GRAPH 3   Age Distribution of New England Graduates, 1851-60

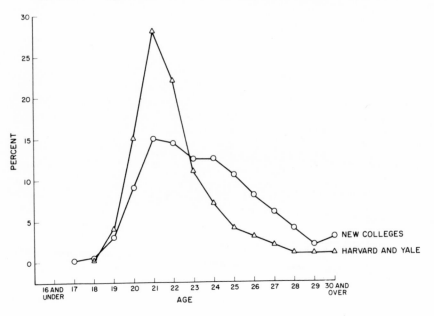

GRAPH 4   Percentage of Graduates Aged 25 or Older, 1751-1900

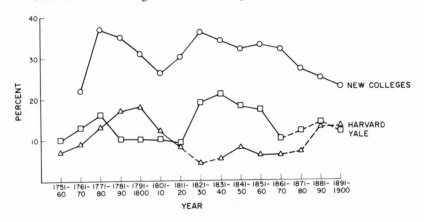

Appendix B

Southampton Students

Students from Southampton have been grouped according to their sources of assistance and ranked according to family wealth, as determined primarily by the town's tax assessment lists. In terms of their sources of support, they fall into three main groups.

Group 1 includes seven students whose families paid all the costs of higher education, without exacting advances against each student's portion of the family estate (see Table 14).

Group 2 includes twenty-eight students whose families provided some aid for their higher education, though not free grants (see Tables 15-17). In contrast to the students in Group 1, these students accepted family aid largely in the form of advances or—in the case of orphans—as their actual portions of family estates. In contrast to those in Group 3, these students apparently received no charitable aid.

Group 3 includes fifteen students who did receive aid from college charitable funds or from education societies (see Table 18). They also may have received aid from their families.

Rankings of family wealth were determined from the Southampton tax lists of 1810, 1821, 1830, and 1840. In most cases, figures on family wealth and acreage came from a tax list within the decade preceding a student's year of graduation; some rankings had to be made on the basis of evidence combined from two lists, however. In determining the total number of taxpayers, I excluded all persons taxed only as polls. In every case, the student's order of birth was based upon the number of children alive in the year of his graduation.

TABLE 14   Group 1: Family-Supported Students

		Graduation		Family		Birth Order	
		Class	Age	Tax Rank	Acres	Son	Child
1.	Isaac Parsons	Yal 11	21	2/214	378	2/2	6/6
2.	Theodore Pomeroy	Yal 08	24	3/214	?	4/4	9/10
3.	Theodore Parsons*	Yal 37	22	5/253	384	1/2	4/7
4.	David Gould	Amh 34	20	6/253	120	1/1	3/6
5.	John Woodbridge	Wms 04	20	5/214	153	1/2	1/3
6.	Henry Edwards	Amh 47	26	9/228	312	1/1	1/3
7.	Jonathan Judd*	Yal 65	21	high	?	1/4	1/7

Note: Figures for birth order include only brothers and sisters alive in the year of each student's graduation. Numbers preceding the slashes under ''son'' and ''child'' refer to the order of a student's birth; numbers following the slashes refer to the total number of living sons and children in the family.

*Theodore Parsons was a nongraduate; Jonathan Judd graduated in 1765.

TABLE 15
Group 2.1: Students Receiving Family Aid
Through Advances on Estates

		Graduation		Family		Birth Order	
		Class	Age	Tax Rank	Acres	Son	Child
		Advances Specifically for Education					
8.	Bela Edwards	Amh 24	22	12/201	175	2/2	4/4
9.	Lewis Clark	Amh 37	25	22/253	206	4/4	6/6
10.	Philetus Clark	Mid 18	24	22/214	139	4/4	5/9
11.	Chandler Bates	Wms 18	32	87/214	39	2/3	3/5
12.	Lemuel Bates	Wms 18	27	87/214	39	3/3	4/5
		Advances Probably for Education					
13.	Lyman Strong	Wms 02	21	18/214	?	3/3	5/5
14.	Federal Burt	Wms 12	24	28/214	173	3/5	5/10
15.	Sylvester Burt	Wms 04	24	28/214	173	1/6	1/10
16.	Israel Searl	Amh 32	22	38/253	155	2/4	5/8
17.	Saul Clark	Wms 05	24	52/214	102	1/2	2/4
18.	Rufus Pomeroy	Wms 08	24	57/214	105	3/5	3/6
19.	Alvan Chapman	Amh 30	21	127/253	?	3/3	4/4
20.	Mahlon Chapman	Amh 32	25	127/253	?	2/3	3/4

TABLE 16
Group 2.2: Students Probably Receiving
Some Family Aid

		Graduation		Family		Birth Order	
		Class	Age	Tax Rank	Acres	Son	Child
21.	Gideon Searl	Uni 30	21	18/253	104	2/4	4/9
22.	Flavius Searle*	Amh 36	22	32/253	100	1/2	2/3
23.	Lemuel Pomeroy	Amh 35	29	46/253	77	2/3	4/7
24.	Justin Clark	Har 16	24	46/214	119	2/3	3/9
25.	Sereno Clark	Amh 35	26	52/253	103	2/2	7/7
26.	Aretas Loomis	Wms 15	25	53/214	?	3/3	4/4
27.	Martin Hurlbut	Wms 04	24	188/214	?	2/4	6/9
28.	Thaddeus Pomeroy	Wms 10	28	?	?	4/4	5/5
29.	Austin Weeks	? 58	26	?	45	?	?

*Flavius Searle was a nongraduate.

TABLE 17
Group 2.3: Students Receiving Family Aid
Through Orphans' Portions

		Graduation		Family		Birth Order	
		Class	Age	Tax Rank	Acres	Son	Child
30.	Jairus Searle	Amh 42	23	10/253	230	2/2	5/8
31.	Joseph Clapp	Amh 29	20	10/214	?	1/1	7/7
32.	Tertius Clark	Yal 24	25	?	?	2/2	2/5
33.	Edward Thorpe	Ham 34	24	18/201	181	2/2	4/6
34.	David Searl*	Dar 84	29	?	100	1/5	1/8
35.	William Strong	Wms 11	26	?	?	2/3	2/4

*David Searl graduated in 1784.

TABLE 18
Group 3: Students Receiving Charity

		Graduation		Family		Birth Order	
		Class	Age	Tax Rank	Acres	Son	Child
36.	Jairus Burt	Amh 24	30	23/201	173	4/5	8/10
37.	Jeremiah Pomeroy	Amh 29	25	27/201	182	3/4	3/7
38.	William Sheldon	Yal 37	21	34/253	?	1/2	2/6
39.	Spencer Clark	Amh 39	24	58/253	61	1/2	1/5
40.	Philander Bates	Amh 33	23	66/253	51	1/4	1/5
41.	Jesse Frary	Amh 31	21	132/253	31	2/5	4/7
42.	Andrew Clapp	Amh 58	25	142/228	24	2/3	2/3
43.	Rufus Hurlbut	Har 13	27	188/214	?	4/4	9/9
44.	Rufus Clapp	Amh 33	25	198/253	?	4/4	7/8
45.	Medad Pomeroy	Wms 17	25	?	?	4/4	7/7
46.	Erastus Clapp	Uni 22	30	?	0	2/3	5/6
47.	Reuben Clapp*	Yal 18	29	?	0	1/3	4/6
48.	Ralph Clapp	Amh 25	30	?	?	3/3	3/4
49.	Abner Clark	Yal 25	29	?	0	2/2	9/9
50.	Justus Janes	Amh 35	27	?	0	?	?

*Reuben Clapp was a nongraduate.

BIBLIOGRAPHIC
ESSAY

Bibliographic Essay

Manuscript Collections

The archives and special collections of New England colleges provided the major portion of manuscript materials for this study. In varying degrees, I used materials in the collections at Amherst, Bowdoin, Dartmouth, Harvard, Middlebury, Vermont, and Yale. Brown, Williams, and Colby have comparable collections. The Amherst College Archives, which I consulted most extensively, contain the whole range of manuscript materials found in other college collections and will serve here as an example of what the rest contain.

For individual Amherst students before 1860, there are folders arranged in class files and containing manuscript letters, diaries, and biographical information. Student societies left numerous record books; I used those of the antislavery societies. The manuscript Student Register (2 vols., 1825-44) lists the absences of each student. The Rank Books (2 vols. for 1829-62), now deposited in the Amherst College Registrar's Office, contain discipline and academic records. Manuscript material on the poor and indigent can be found in records kept by the college on its own charity fund and on A.E.S. beneficiaries, the latter in a series of record books and notebooks that contain lists of names and appropriations for almost the whole nineteenth century. College financial records also contain information on students; see especially the term-bill ledgers and treasurer's records. Amherst Faculty Records (in four bound volumes for 1825-60) contain minutes of all meetings and much detail on discipline and government. See also various documents in bound volumes of Amherst College Memorabilia. I found materials dealing with my particular interests arranged in comparable groups at other college archives.

For education societies, the most important manuscript sources are in the archives of the American Education Society, Congregational Library, Boston. This large collection of correspondence, records, and other papers constitutes an incomparable body of material on benevolent movements and on poor students. It had not been examined by other scholars when I first used it; it has since been arranged. Of special importance for this study were the following materials: Beneficiary Account Book, with names of beneficiaries numbered 1 through 2,700; Letter Books, 3 vols., 1826-54, containing copies of letters from the secretary; Beneficiary Letters, 1828-54; and a society record book with the original constitution and minutes of annual meetings, 1815-74.

Records of the Maine Branch and of the Worcester County Religious Charitable Society are also in this collection. Archives of the Hampshire Education Society are in Forbes Library, Northampton, Mass.

Southampton materials were found mainly in the Treasurer-Collector's Office, Southampton, Mass. (tax assessment lists, town records); in Forbes Library, Northampton (genealogies, vital records, church records); and in the Hampshire County Probate Registry, Hall of Records, Northampton, Mass. (wills and probate records). For individual items, see the notes to Chapter 1.

Published Primary Sources

A surprisingly large body of college institutional records has been published in document collections. Most helpful for this study were *Harvard College Records*, vols. 1 and 2 edited by Albert Matthews (Boston, 1925), and vol. 3 edited by Samuel Eliot Morison (Boston, 1935). These three volumes appear in the Publications of the Colonial Society of Massachusetts, vols. 15, 16, and 31. Written histories of the colleges published in the nineteenth century also contain many primary documents.

College catalogs after 1820 began to include information on costs, financial assistance, food, lodging, and work; they also listed the names and residences of students, the calendar, the faculty, and the curriculum. The college archives have kept complete files of their catalogs, and many New England libraries have partial sets. I have examined catalogs for all institutions included in this study.

Biographical registers published by the colleges contain an immense amount of material on graduates, as do the class books. Sketches in the class books usually provide most detail; these publications began with graduating classes of the early nineteenth century, but there were occasional lapses through the 1850s. The biographical registers make it possible to study the age structure, career patterns, and geographical distribution of the college population.

I used the following registers in determining ages of graduates: Louise Bauer and William T. Hastings, comps., *The Historical Catalogue of Brown University, 1764-1934* (Providence, R.I.: Brown University, 1936); Charles P. Chipman, comp., *General Catalogue of Officers, Graduates and Former Students of Colby College* (Waterville, Me.: Colby College, 1920); *Dartmouth College and Associated Schools: General Catalogue, 1769-1940* (Hanover, N.H.: Dartmouth College Publications, 1940); Calvin Durfee, *Williams Biographical Annals* (Boston: Lee and Shepard, 1871); J. E. Goodrich, comp., *General Catalogue of the University of Vermont and State Agricultural College, 1791-1900* (Burlington, Vt.: Free Press Association, 1901); William L. Montague, ed., *Biographical Record of the Alumni of Amherst College, During Its First Half Century, 1821-1871* (Amherst, Mass.: J. E. Williams, 1883); Philip S. Wilder, ed., *General Catalogue of Bowdoin College, 1794-1950* (Brunswick, Me.: Anthoensen Press, 1950); and Edgar J. Wiley, comp., *Catalogue of the Officers and Students of Middlebury College, 1800-1927* (Middlebury, Vt.: Middlebury College, 1928). These registers provided evidence for all graduating classes at provincial colleges for the period of this study; most institutions have issued volumes in addition to the ones cited here.

For Harvard and Yale there are gaps in the published evidence. I used Clifford K. Shipton, *Sibley's Harvard Graduates*, through vol. 14 (Boston: Massachusetts Historical Society, 1968), which reaches the class of 1760. I gathered age data on classes between 1751 and 1860 from the manuscript Records of the College Faculty in the Harvard University Archives, and from class books, also in the archives. For Yale, I used Franklin B. Dexter, *Biographical Sketches of the Graduates of Yale College, with Annals of the College History*, through vol. 6 (New Haven: Yale University Press, 1912), which covers all classes through 1815. Evidence on classes between 1816 and 1860 came from class books in the Yale University Archives.

Education society publications cover almost the whole of the nineteenth century and are deposited in many New England college libraries. The Congregational Library in Boston has a large collection. Most important for this study were the annual reports of the American Education Society, 1816-74, and the society's *American Quarterly Register*, 15 vols. (1827-43), available on microfilm in the American Periodical Series, reels 532-34. Local education societies and branches of the A.E.S. also published annual reports.

Student manuals, diaries, letters, autobiographies, and biographies also provided primary material. For specific references, see notes to the text.

Secondary Works

Writings by other historians on individual colleges, higher education, and the history of New England society are cited throughout the text. For detailed listings of other works on the history of colleges, universities, and higher education, see the following: Joe Park, ed., *The Rise of American Education: An Annotated Bibliography* (Evanston, Ill.: Northwestern University Press, 1965); Bernard Bailyn, *Education in the Forming of American Society* (Chapel Hill, N.C.: University of North Carolina Press, 1960), pp. 53-136; George E. Peterson, *The New England College in the Age of the University* (Amherst, Mass.: Amherst College Press, 1964), pp. 239-52; Frederick Rudolph, *The American College and University: A History* (New York: Alfred A. Knopf, 1962), pp. 497-516; and Laurence R. Veysey, *The Emergence of the American University* (Chicago: University of Chicago Press, 1965), pp. 448-62.

Suggestions for research in problems of philanthropy can be found in Merle Curti and Roderick Nash, *Philanthropy in the Shaping of American Higher Education* (New Brunswick, N.J.: Rutgers University Press, 1965), and in Wilbur K. Jordan's three studies, *The Charities of London, 1480-1660* (1960), *The Charities of Rural England, 1480-1660* (1961), and *Philanthropy in England, 1480-1660* (1959)—all published in London by George Allen & Unwin.

Guides to methods in demographic history can be found in E. A. Wrigley, ed., *An Introduction to English Historical Demography* (New York: Basic Books, 1966). See also Peter Laslett, *The World we have lost* (New York: Charles Scribner's Sons, 1965); and Lawrence Stone, ''Prosopography,''

Daedalus: Historical Studies Today 100, no. 1 (1971): 46-79. For New England studies, see Philip J. Greven, Jr., "Historical Demography and Colonial America," *William and Mary Quarterly*, 3d ser. 24 (1967): 438-54; Kenneth A. Lockridge, *A New England Town: The First Hundred Years* (New York: W. W. Norton & Company, 1970), especially pp. 181-99; and John Demos, *A Little Commonwealth: Family Life in Plymouth Colony* (New York: Oxford University Press, 1970).

In the social history of education and the student population, a modern work has made major advances: Philippe Aries, *Centuries of Childhood: A Social History of Family Life*, trans. Robert Baldick (New York: Alfred A. Knopf, 1962). A series of new essays on students in England and Scotland has appeared in *Past and Present*: see Mark Curtis, "The Alienated Intellectuals of Early Stuart England," no. 23 (1962), pp. 25-43; Joan Simon, "The Social Origins of Cambridge Students, 1603-1640," no. 26 (1963), pp. 58-67; Lawrence Stone, "The Educational Revolution in England, 1560-1640," no. 28 (1964), pp. 41-80; W. M. Mathew, "The Origins and Occupations of Glasgow Students, 1740-1839," no. 33 (1966), pp. 74-94; and David Cressy, "Communication: The Social Composition of Caius College, Cambridge, 1580-1640," no. 47 (1970), pp. 113-15. See also Mark Curtis, *Oxford and Cambridge in Transition, 1558-1642* (Oxford, England: Clarendon Press, 1959); and Hugh Kearney, *Scholars and Gentlemen: Universities and Society in Pre-Industrial Britain, 1500-1700* (Ithaca, N.Y.: Cornell University Press, 1970).

For an exemplary treatment of family expenditure for education, see Joseph A. Banks, *Prosperity and Parenthood: A Study of Family Planning among the Victorian Middle Classes* (London: Routledge & Kegan Paul Limited, 1954), pp. 170-96. For an analysis of the significance of changes in community patterns, life sequences, and routines, see Eric Lampard, "Urbanization and Social Change; on Broadening the Scope and Relevance of Urban History," in *The Historian and the City*, ed. Oscar Handlin and John Burchard (Cambridge, Mass.: M.I.T. Press and Harvard University Press, 1963), pp. 225-47. I found Lampard's essay particularly helpful in writing Chapters 2 and 6, where his ideas for writing the social history of cities seemed to apply equally to colleges and students.

INDEX

Index